Looking at
North Lancashire

D1476769

40p.

Uniform with this volume:
Looking at CENTRAL LANCASHIRE
Looking at SOUTH LANCASHIRE

Other Dalesman books on Lancashire:
BOWLAND AND PENDLE HILL
CLITHEROE AND THE RIBBLE VALLEY
GRANGE AND CARTMEL
LANCASHIRE RECIPES
UNDERGROUND IN FURNESS

Looking at
North Lancashire

by
"Spartina"

A 39557
914.272

THE DALESMAN PUBLISHING CO., LTD.
Clapham (Via Lancaster)
Yorkshire

First Published 1971

© "Spartina" 1971

Printed by Galava Printing Co., Ltd., Hallam Road, Nelson, Lancs.

Contents

"Spartina" is a group of four Lancashire authors; D. Pilling, M. Thompson, D. Tibbitt and D. Underwood; they would like to thank all those persons who have so willingly supplied information and without whose help this book would not have been possible. The illustrations are by Harry Pilling, the front cover photograph of Hornby Castle is by David Joy, and the map on the back cover is by Janet Ellerington.

Introduction

IN these books, which we hope will be of as much interest to the resident as the visitor, we have tried to dispel the myth that Lancashire is the ugly sister of the North, dull and uninteresting. We hope you will be interested to read of ghosts and witches, the legends associated with them, and the fine abbeys, churches and mansions with which Lancashire abounds. Delve into the past at one of the many museums and examine unique collections of dolls, aircraft and railway engines; try some of the county dishes and see where they are made; or take part in some of the more unusual sports and hobbies or local customs. Take a lazy trip down one of the many canals, search for the wild life or go fishing. Explore the docks and harbours and watch the fishing fleet sail out to sea, following a channel taken by the Vikings many years ago. Lancashire holds many treasures, old and new. It is a county which gives a little of everything—sea and mountain, cities and small hamlets, and each has a place to explore.

1:   A Short History of Lancashire

LANCASHIRE and its peoples have lived through many changes from the invasion of the Romans to the invasion of the Industrial Revolution. The county accepted each new influx of men and ideas and absorbed them into its pattern, and it is this pattern which can be rediscovered today in "Looking at Lancashire."

Roman conquest of Britain began in 43 A.D. and it was sixteen years later that the conquest of the North West began, the Romans crossing the Mersey at Latchford and proceeding across the Ribble. The tribe of Brigantes lived in Northern England and they were used by the Roman soldiers to build roads and the garrisons at Ribchester (Brenetennacum) and Manchester (Mancunium). Excavations have revealed a considerable number of Roman objects: inscribed altar stones, coins, jewelry and pottery. A bronze helmet was found at Ribchester in 1796, a bronze bust of Minerva at Warrington and the remains of an altar at Wigan.

When the Angles came into Lancashire from Yorkshire, Northumberland and Durham in about 570 A.D., some settled in the valleys of the Lune and Ribble until the 11th century. The population of Angles increased, names such as Wigan, Treales and Makerfield date back to this period. There have been a few Anglo-Saxon finds; coins at Little Crosby near Liverpool and at Heaton Moor near Lancaster. A chest containing ingots of silver and 10,000 silver coins was found at Cuerdale, near Preston in 1840, and was known as the "Cuerdale Hoard". Some of these coins were Danish and some were of the period of Alfred the Great and his son, Edward the Elder. The Danish invasion of Lancashire began with isolated raids, but evidence of settlement is shown in such names as Hulme, Davyhulme, Levenshulme, Oldham, Flixton and Urmston in the Manchester area. About 900 Norsemen settled in the county and the names Scales, Scarisbrick and Norbreck are Norse, while those of Goosnargh and Grimsargh are of half Irish-Norse descent. Norse crosses have been found at Whalley, Lancaster, Bolton, Winwick, Halton and Urswick. They consist of a circle between the arms of the cross, and are usually of stone and carved with snake and chain decorations. Norse tombs, known as hogsbacks, are to be found at Heysham and Bolton-le-Sands. Edward the Elder and

Aethelflaed, children of Alfred the Great, built forts at Thelwall
and Runcorn, while the land between the Ribble and the Mersey
was a royal domain until after the Norman Conquest. The Domesday
Book states that at this time Lancashire was wooded, with scattered
farmsteads and vast areas of rough grassland.

During the reign of William I, the county was administered by the
King's cousin, Roger of Poitou, who chose Lancaster as the site for
his castle. This was the beginning of Lancashire's close connection
with the Royal family. In the 15th century the confiscated lands of
the supporters of Lambert Simnel, pretender to the throne, were
given to Lord Strange, son of the Earl of Derby. These gifts included
estates in Wigan, Bury, Salford and Manchester, estates south of
the Ribble and the Broughton estates in Furness and Cartmel, and
thus the Derby family became the richest and most important in
Lancashire. The Earldom of Derby has played a prominent part in
the county throughout the centuries, King Henry VIII and Queen
Elizabeth I having stayed at Knowsley Hall, home of the Earls of
Derby.

In the reign of Elizabeth I, Lancashire was the strongest Catholic
county, although Manchester and Bolton were strongholds of
Puritanism. Religious belief was the deciding factor in the Civil
War; in 1642 Lord Derby led the Royalists and some years later
Cromwell marched down the Ribble valley and gained control of
Preston. Later Lord Derby's army was defeated and he was taken
prisoner, tried and executed in 1651. During Jacobite times there was
dissension and plotting, the Lancashire Jacobites encouraging the
Scottish Jacobites to invade England by way of Lancashire. This
they did in 1715, but were defeated. The next attempt was in 1745
when Bonnie Prince Charlie with his troops came to Lancaster,
Preston and Manchester, planning to march to London, but at
Derby he abandoned the march and returned to Preston. In Tudor
and Stuart times the population of Lancashire was small, but there
were great industrial developments. By the 18th century more people
were coming into the county, and with the Industrial Revolution
the problem of poverty was rife. It was during this time that
Lancashire's cotton industry came to the fore and her trade steadily
increased. Mills, coal mines, factories and docks covered large
areas. The opening of the Manchester Ship Canal in 1894, the
construction of the East Lancashire road in the 1920s and the making
of the Mersey Tunnel in 1934 greatly improved communications.

Lancashire with its industrial regions is one of the mainsprings of
Britain's commerce. Manchester is the centre of the cotton industry
and electrical engineering. St. Helens, largest producer of glass in
the world, also has large chemical factories, copper foundries and
cable works. Liverpool is one of the world's great trading centres
with its docks, shipyards and airport.

Traditional Foods

THERE is an old Lancashire saying: "Trouble is naught, cost is all". The people of Lancashire suffered hardship and poverty during the years of the Industrial Revolution and it may be that this was the reason for the traditional foods of the county being cheap, appetising, nourishing, easily prepared and easily obtained. Most families, if fortunate enough to be in employment, were working in the mills, factories and local coal mines, and would buy food on the way home from work. The corner shop and small home bakeries were the source of many traditional foods.

Flookburgh Mussels. Flookburgh is situated at the end of the Cartmel peninsula. Centuries ago the coaches stopped here on their journey across the sands and so it became an important place. Flook means fluke—a plaice, burgh (or town)—and the name is appropriate as fluking, shrimping and cockling have been the town's mainstay for many years. The Vikings made a settlement here in the tenth century. Flookburgh fluke and mussels are well known throughout Britain, and it is interesting to note that the weathervane on the church tower is in the form of a fluke. In 1675 King Charles, who granted a Royal Charter to the town, dined at the Crown Inn on a "feast of cockles". The original case carrying the great seal of England, and resplendent in royal purple embossed in leather, is in the Flookburgh Church. Also to be seen are ancient market regalia and two halberd heads, one in the shape of a fluke. The people of Flookburgh certainly respected their mussels and flukes.

Heysham Nettle Beer is a traditional home-made beer and, as nettles are easily obtained in this area, it has been brewed for many years. About two gallons or 1 peck of nettles are needed to the same quantity of water, 4 lbs malt, 4 ozs. sarsparilla, $\frac{1}{2}$ oz. root ginger, 1 oz. yeast, 2 ozs. hops, $1\frac{1}{2}$ lbs. sugar. The nettles are washed, put into a large saucepan with the water, ginger, malt, hops and sarsaparilla, and then brought to the boil and boiled for 15 minutes. The sugar is put into a large pan or earthenware jar and the strained nettle mixture is poured on to it. This is stirred until all the sugar is dissolved. The yeast is beaten to a cream with a little sugar, which is then put into the nettle mixture and left until it begins to ferment.

A Morecambe Bay shrimper

After this it has to be carefully bottled and the corks wired down. String is not effective because the gas will cause the tops to blow off if not securely held. The beer can be drunk immediately but is a better flavour if kept several weeks.

Lancashire Cheese is a popular and rich delicacy. It can be bought either mild or "tasty", the latter being of a strong flavour. In spite of competition from continental and fancy cheeses, Lancashire cheese is still a firm favourite and can be found in all the grocery shops and markets. Cheese and pickled onions are available in country inns throughout the county, while cheese and apple pie are traditional Lancashire fare which go well together.

Lancashire Hot Pot is an economical dish made from potatoes, onions and cheap cuts of lamb or mutton. It is left in the oven to cook slowly for many hours and requires little attention. Traditionally it is cooked in a brown earthenware dish with a plate on top.

Morecambe Bay Prawns and Shrimps. In the waters of Morecambe Bay many succulent crustacea and fish are to be found, shrimps, mussels, whitebait, flukes and plaice being in abundance. As these are in demand, an industry has built up in the area. Early each morning, before the tide turns fishermen are out with a horse and cart to gather the shrimps, mussels and cockles. Huge nets are dragged across the shallow water and the big wheels of the cart are almost covered. Shrimps are the most popular catch. These are boiled and picked before being packed in a factory where they are weighed, placed in cartons and covered with melted butter flavoured with herbs and spices. The cartons are then sent to the shops and are a popular food. Some fishermen still net fluke and plaice, but the demand for them has decreased.

Tripe is another popular dish in the county. Lancashire tripe is bleached and cooked and can be eaten cold as bought. Tripe and onions is made by cooking the tripe in milk and then adding a sauce made from cooked onions, cornflour and milk. This is very nourishing and cheap. Tripe on a skewer used to be sold in Bolton at the fair every January 1st, together with black peas.

Trotters of pigs and the feet of sheep are boiled and skinned, cooked with onions and served with a white sauce made from the stock, or eaten cold.

3:   Legends, Ghosts and Witches

The dead man's hand

SOMEWHERE in the north of the county, according to legend, there once lived a girl whose name was Ellen. Her parents had died when she was young and she was now very wealthy. Ellen loved her cousin but he was a Catholic and she was not, and he went away to the wars not knowing of her love. Her maid Bridget was also a Catholic, and when Ellen became seriously ill with fever she prayed for her mistress's recovery.

One night Ellen dreamed she saw a priest, whose right hand was missing, standing by her bed. Bridget saw this as a sign, and she brought to Ellen an old woman who claimed to be a prophetess. The woman drew a circle on the floor, and within the circle a human hand. That night Ellen had another strange dream; she saw the hand pointing to a house where she felt she would be cured. Immediately Ellen and Bridget set off to find this house. After four days travelling they again met the old woman who led them to a gatehouse which Ellen recognised as the one in her dream. They knocked at the door and asked for a priest, and they were told that this was Bryn Hall and there was a priest who would see them. The priest showed them a human hand, a saintly relic, preserved and kept in a white silk bag. This would cure Ellen of her fever and she was put to bed with the hand on her heart. Ellen did indeed recover from her fever and she was invited to stay with Lady Gerard, the owner of Bryn Hall.

Ellen was told that there was a magic mirror at the Hall where she could see her true love. She was taken to a dark room and a light was directed on to what appeared to be a mirror—in it she saw her cousin William and then the old woman who turned out to be William in disguise. Ellen discovered this had been a plot between Bridget, William and Lady Gerard. Being devout Catholics, they had believed the hand would cure Ellen of her fever. The mirror, really an opening in the wall, was a trick to convince Ellen that William loved her, and a few weeks later they were married.

Bryn Hall, long since demolished, was the ancient home of the Gerard family about the year 1280. When the family left the house, a Roman Catholic priest remained behind who had in his care a human hand. The hand was preserved in a white silk bag and was claimed to be the cure for countless ills. It was said to be the hand of Father Arrowsmith, a priest who was hanged in Lancaster for his beliefs. The hand of a dead person was widely believed to possess great healing powers. It had to be taken as soon as possible after death, and people would bribe executioners to give them the hands of the condemned. Failing this it was not uncommon for people to go at night to the gibbet where bodies were left and remove a hand.

George Fox

THIS old Lancashire legend is said to have its origins in the year 1652. It tells of two travellers who were trying to reach Cartmel from Kendal, but had lost their way in a mountain fog. One of them was George Fox, the founder of the Quakers. It seemed that they would have to spend the night on the bleak wet moors, and they had settled down on some dry rocks when the mist began to disperse. Fox told his companion, Ralph Seaton, that they would move on, and going down the hill they followed a stream until they reached a tavern. Here they found two rough looking men drinking and eating. The inn was guarded by a fierce watch-dog.

As Fox and Seaton entered, a woman with coarse mannish features shouted at the dog which slunk into a corner. Near the fire sat a man who appeared to be insane. Seaton put down the case he was carrying, and the woman told two men to carry it to a room kept specially for travellers. Seaton felt very uneasy, although George Fox seemed unaware of the fact. The woman went to a cupboard and brought out a "flesh pie" for their supper, but as Seaton cut into the pie his attention was caught by the man sitting by the fire. He imagined the man gave him a sign not to eat, and so he refused. George Fox took a large helping, but after two mouthfulls asked if he might have bacon instead.

After the meal, the travellers said they were tired. The woman, taking them outside, showed them to a room in the roof entered by a ladder. Once upstairs in the cold and dirty room, Seaton and Fox realised they were to be robbed and murdered and there seemed no way of escape. Suddenly a shower of pebbles was thrown at the barred window and outside in the yard they saw the man who had appeared insane. He motioned them to remove the bars and make their escape, and this they did. Fox and Seaton then crossed the nearby river, and soon heard horses and the baying of a hound. From where they were hiding, they saw three horsemen and the dog from the inn. The next morning George Fox said they must return to the tavern, although Seaton was most reluctant to do so. When they reached it, they found several horses tied up outside and explained to the strangers resting there what had happened the previous night. A search revealed a hoard of stolen money and ample proof that other travellers had been murdered. Eventually the old woman and the other men were captured and punished. The man who was insane was the son of the old woman; he had times of lucidity and it was during one such period that he had warned the travellers to escape. Fox and Seaton ensured that he was properly looked after and his life made as tolerable as possible.

George Fox was the founder of the Quakers and in 1652 he came to the Ulverston district to preach. He visited Swarthmoor Hall which was the home of Judge Fell. After convincing the judge of his beliefs a service was held at the Hall every Sunday. Judge Fell died soon afterwards and eventually George Fox married his widow. The Quakers, or Friends as they were originally called, got their name when one of their number was taken to court. Telling the people present to tremble before the name of the Lord, they were thus referred to as "Quakers".

The Trial of the Lancashire Witches

WITCH hunting in England became almost a mania during the reign of King James I. It was during this time that the Lancashire witches from the Pendle Forest area were caught and sent for trial at Lancaster Castle. Between 1542 and 1735 approximately 1,000 witches were executed in this country.

The Lancashire witches were renowned for their spiteful and revengeful spells, for wasting cattle and ruining crops. The ringleaders were Elizabeth Southern (Old Demdike) and Anne Whittle (Old Chattox), who were both very old women. Their covens were made up of members of their families plus a few neighbours. A few years before their trial the two families argued and this ultimately was their downfall. After the argument, Chattox and Demdike each tried to outdo the other, both claiming to be the more powerful and openly admitting to be the cause of several mysterious deaths in the district.

According to legend, Demdike in 1591 met the devil disguised as a small boy in the Forest of Pendle. She sold her soul to him and he then appeared in the form of her familiar, a small brown dog called Tibb. One day after this meeting the witch was walking over a farmer's field with her grand-daughter, Alison Device. The farmer shouted at them and ordered them both off his land. At this Demdike turned to the farmer and told him to go and hang himself. The following day the farmer's son fell ill, and a year later he died, his death being attributed to Demdike's dog, Tibb.

In 1612 Demdike was brought before the magistrates, the authorities having now heard of her evil doings. Demdike condemned her grand-daughter, Alison Device, and Old Chattox, who were accused of murdering Robert Nutter a local farmer. The three were then taken to Lancaster Castle and imprisoned. On Good

Friday following the arrests, Elizabeth Device called a meeting at the Malkin Tower in Pendle Forest and a plot was laid to kill the Governor and blow up Lancaster Castle. Then the two families, their feud forgotten, held a feast together, arranging to meet again in a year's time. However, the magistrates heard of this meeting and immediately arrested nine of the twenty people who had been present, the rest fleeing.

The trial began in August 1612. The chief witnesses were Demdike's grand-children, James and Jennet Device, although eventually Jennet betrayed James and he too was executed. Elizabeth Device was condemned by her daughter Jennet, then a child of nine. In 1634 Jennet herself was accused of witchcraft and brought to trial. Ten of the accused were executed including Chattox; her daughter Anne Redfearn; Elizabeth Device, daughter of Demdike; and Elizabeth's two children, Alison (aged eleven), and James. Alice Nutter, mother of the murdered farmer Robert Nutter, was also accused by the Device family, found guilty and executed. Execution for witches ranged from decapitation to being burned at the stake. If a witch renounced her confession, the worst crime of all, she was slowly burned alive over green wood. Old Demdike is supposed to have died on her way to the stake, but was nevertheless burned.

The Ghosts of Levens Hall

LEVENS HALL, on the banks of the river Kent, has numerous ghosts. One of these is known as the Grey Lady, and according to legend is supposed to be a gypsy woman who came to the house begging for food and shelter. She was refused admittance and died of starvation, but before dying foretold that no son should inherit the house until the river Kent ceased to flow and a white fawn was born in the park. This seemed unlikely as the deer in the park at Levens Hall are black fallow deer, although in fact their colour is very dark brown. However, both these events occurred at the time of the birth of Alan Desmond Bagot, a white fawn being discovered in the park and the river Kent freezing. It is not known whether the story of the gypsy's curse is true, but the Grey Lady has made many appearances at the Hall.

The Pink Lady, a woman dressed in a pink print dress and mob cap, also appears for no apparent reason. The Black Dog is the most frequent apparition to be seen; it is a large and woolly dog which appears to run in front of visitors to Levens Hall. Many guests, seeing the animal run up the stairs before them, have searched in vain for him. Apart from these occurrences, Mr. R. Bagot, the present owner, has been seen and heard playing the harpsichord at Levens Hall when in fact he was in Keswick.

(See Levens Hall, p. 28)

The Luck of Muncaster

ALTHOUGH this legend took place just outside the borders of the county, it concerns a Lancashire family and is considered to be one of Lancashire's legends. The story is about the Pennington family who originally lived in the village of the same name, mid-way between Dalton and Ulverston. The first member of the family on record was Gamel de Pennington who, about forty years before the Conquest, left Lancashire to live at Muncaster.

The Henry VI room in the castle is where this legend begins in 1461. At this time the building was the home of Sir John Pennington, who one day found the King hiding in a wood near the Castle and gave him food and refuge from his enemies. When the King left he gave Sir John a glass cup, studded with gold and white enamel spots. Before presenting it, he crossed himself with water from the cup and told the family they would prosper as long as it remained unbroken. The superstition of those times thought that good luck would pass to Sir John's descendants, and the cup was called "The Luck of Muncaster."

The family, determined to keep the cup safe, secretly buried it. When the war was over the family decided to disinter the cup, but unfortunately the box containing it was dropped and it was forty years before anyone dared to open the box to determine its safety. They need not have feared, for the cup was intact and the family happily proclaimed the safety of "The Luck of Muncaster."

The Peel of Fouldrey

THE ancient castle of Peel of Fouldrey is the scene of this old Lancashire legend. In 1487, the Pretender and an army, which was planning to overthrow Henry VII, landed on the island and took it from the monks of Furness. The island was deserted except for one or two fishermen's cottages and a castle, beneath which ran a passage said to have been the scene of a gruesome murder and supposedly haunted. The ghost had been seen by Dick, one of the fishermen on the island.

One night loud cries were heard from the royal room at the castle and the pretender, obviously terrified, said he had seen a dark figure in his room. The next morning Sir Thomas Broughton arrived to draw up the plans for the battle, when suddenly with a loud cry he disappeared through a hole in the floor. In the opening appeared the fisherman, Dick, who had been exploring the haunted passage-way and had undone a trap door. Dick was taken to the dungeons.

Later there arrived at the castle a messenger from the Abbot of Furness who had previously been warned that here was not the real pretender, Edward, Earl of Warwick, but a man called Lambert Simnel. A priest called Simon then offered to prove by supernatural means that this was the real pretender. He stamped on the floor and suddenly the whole building shook violently; he then put his foot down gently and the room was filled with a thick white mist. The assembly dispersed and the monk hurried off to report to the Abbot.

The disturbances terrified the guards who were holding Dick and they fled, leaving the fisherman to escape to the top of the castle where he remained until darkness fell. Attempting to make his way down, he mistakenly went to the pretender's bedroom. The priest Simon, unable to see him, took him to be a pre-arranged messenger and gave him a package, and Dick then made his way out of the castle to where a boat was waiting. As he could not read, he decided to take the packet to the Abbot at Furness who looked at the contents and realised that treachery was being planned against the king. He sent a warning, and then laid a plan to lure the revolutionaries away from the island.

That night Dick appeared in the priest Simon's bedroom at the castle. The priest, only half awake, was terrified, but then suddenly a gruesome spectre appeared and picked Dick up around the waist. It told the priest that the fisherman had betrayed them all and they must leave the castle, and it then went up the stairs to the turret carrying Dick. The spectre threw his body down to the water below and then vanished. The next day the troops left Fouldrey and camped near Ulverston, but the rebellion gained no supporters and the rebels were forced to move south. At Newark they engaged in battle with the King's men. The principal leaders of the plot were killed, and it is said that as the priest Simon was dying on the battlefield the gruesome spectre appeared before him again to taunt him of his failure to overthrow the King. Simnel the pretender was pardoned and sent to work in the Royal kitchens.

Raven Castle

NOTHING now remains of Raven Castle which stood on the border of Lancashire and Yorkshire near the Trough of Bowland. This legend is said to date some time in the 16th century. The castle was then owned by Hildebrand Wentworth who had summoned two highwaymen, Michael and Anthony. While Michael spoke privately to Hildebrand, Anthony was told by a servant that the owner had in his care the two children of Sir Henry Fairfax. Their father had been killed at the wars, and their mother was presumed to have committed suicide as her clothes had been found by the river. Her ghost was still said to walk in the wood, and Anthony remembered a ghostly figure which had crossed their path twice on the way—a sure omen of death. The two children, Julia and Geoffrey, were looked after at the castle by their faithful nurse Alice. When Michael had been told by Hildebrand where to take the children they set off. They rode for some time until Anthony knew they were on the Ingleton road, for he could hear the river. Then he realised that they were to murder the children. This he refused to do, and he and Michael fought until eventually Michael was thrown over a bridge into the waterfall below.

Hildebrand meanwhile spent that day in his room at the castle. At last he was master of all. Suddenly a figure in a dark robe appeared and he recognised Lady Fairfax, who was standing before a small cabinet which contained deeds Sir Henry had given him. These placed the children and all Sir Henry's possessions into Hildebrand's care on the death of Lady Fairfax. At the sight of the "ghost," Hildebrand fell to the floor. The following morning he complained of feeling ill and again stayed in his room. His servant told him that a messenger had arrived with the news that Sir Henry was not dead, but only a prisoner, and that the deeds from the cabinet would prove his identity and release him. Hildebrand told the messenger to wait outside and then went to the cabinet but the deeds had gone. Seizing this opportunity, he forged a new set of deeds making Sir Henry a traitor. He sealed them up and the messenger departed.

Everything was now planned but Hildebrand was restless. He had not heard if the children were dead, and at last he went to the waterfall and crossed the bridge to a ruined keep on the far side of the river. Here he found the children with their nurse Alice. In fury he drew his sword, but before he could strike them Lady Faifrax appeared and Hildebrand fled. On leaving the ruin he was met by two horsemen, one being Sir Henry who ordered to be taken to the children. Hildebrand then threw himself off the bridge and was drowned, while Sir Henry and his family were united. Later it was learned that Hildebrand had threatened Lady Fairfax, and so she had planned her apparent suicide after leaving the children in Alice's care. When the messenger had arrived at the castle, Lady Fairfax had been warned by Alice, stolen the deeds and given them to the messenger.

The Ring and the Cliff

THE Lancashire coast—probably a high ridge above Broughton-in-Furness—is supposed to be the setting for this legend. Two lovers, Adeline and Mortimer, were to part when Mortimer left on a ship which was lying at anchor off the coast. Mortimer gave Adeline a ring and begged her to wait for him, saying that a curse would fall on her if she did not. Adeline gave him a lock of her hair, but did not promise to be true. Some years later a ship again anchored off the coast and a man came ashore. It was Mortimer who had returned to make Adeline his wife. Passing the tavern he approached a small house and heard Adeline singing a ballad he had once taught her. After knocking on the door he asked the servants if their mistress was at home, and then Adeline appeared. Mortimer asked her to marry him, but she shrank back and said that she was already married. Mortimer was heart broken and returned to the tavern where he was taken ill with fever.

One December evening Adeline was sitting on the cliffs alone, for she was certain that Mortimer would return for her. But only her husband found her and brutally returned her to the house. For a while she was imprisoned, but gradually this was relaxed and again she was left to herself. Once again she went to the cliffs taking with her the ring that Mortimer had given her, certain that this time he would come for her. Thinking she heard his boat on the water, she leapt from the cliffs to her death.

The cliff, now called "The Lady's Cliff," is said to be still haunted by Adeline's unhappy spirit, while the ring was virtually undamaged and was kept by her family. Mortimer recovered from the fever and lived to be an old man. Every day he would walk to the cliffs and downcast would sit there before returning to his home. When he died he was buried in the churchyard, and a plain stone with the initials CM still marks the spot called the "Stranger's Grave."

Sambo's Grave

A T Sunderland Point, near Heysham, can still be seen the grave of Sambo, a poor slave. This is a reminder of the old trading days when slaves were brought ashore here to be smuggled secretly to the large wealthy houses in the Lake District. According to legend, Sambo was a faithful slave from the West Indies. In 1763 his master, a sea captain, had business in Lancaster and left him at Sunderland Point without informing him of his whereabouts. Thinking his master had deserted him, poor Sambo pined away and died. His grave is still to be seen and the epitaph on his tombstone opens with these lines:—

> *Full sixty years the angry winter's wave,*
> *Has thundering dash'd this bleak and barren shore,*
> *Since Sambo's head laid in this lonely grave,*
> *Lies still and ne'er will hear their turmoil more.*

The "cotton tree" said to have been planted by Sambo still grows here. Sunderland Point can be reached by walking across the tidal road from Overton, but first check the time of high tide.

4: Places of Interest

Furness Abbey, Barrow-in-Furness.
Route: A6, A590. Grounds always open to the public.

IN 1124 a small monastic house was erected on the north bank of the river Ribble near Tulketh. Built by Stephen, later King of England, it was given to the Carthusian Order and was intended as a living for thirteen monks. It was later decided that a larger site should be found for a new monastery. The monks moved to the promontory abutting Morecambe Bay where work began on Furness Abbey in 1127. The Abbey is situated in a most beautifully wooded valley known as "Bekansgill," a name which is believed to mean Vale of the Deadly Nightshade.

In the 13th century the Carthusian Order amassed great wealth, and the abbey was richly endowed with estates at Furness and the neighbouring island of Walney. The wealth and influence of the Abbot was such that toward the end of the 13th century he possessed lands as far afield as Cumberland, Lincolnshire and the Isle of Man. He also owned ships and concerned himself with trading in iron ore, and at one point a castle was built at nearby Dalton to act as a defence in case the abbey was attacked.

Such activities hardly seemed in keeping with the strict rules and disciplines of the Carthusian Order, and such was the corrupting influence of power, finance and trading that in later years the Abbot had almost assumed the role of a temporal monarch. The state of affairs became so lax that one Abbot, rumour has it, had two wives while one of the monks had acquired five wives. The Dissolution of the Monasteries brought an abrupt end to the life of Furness Abbey. A rising against the dissolution was organised in 1536 but was soon put down by the officers of the king and many of the monks were killed. By 1537 the Abbey was finally dissolved.

Today the abbey stands in ruins. Built of soft red sandstone, much of the structure is badly weathered and eroded by time, but even so Furness Abbey is one of the finest monastic ruins in the country. The church was some 275 feet in length and in places these walls can be seen to be over five feet thick. While much of the fabric is of the 12th century there was extensive rebuilding in the 15th

Furness Abbey

century, particularly of the east end, transept and belfry tower. Remains of dormitories, cloisters and refectory are still standing, and of particular interest is a very fine sedilia in one wall of the choir. There is also a 14th century infirmary chapel which has been turned into a small museum showing many relevant exhibits.

The Trough of Bowland

IT comes as a pleasant surprise to visitors to Lancashire to find a wild upland region on the edge of the Forest of Bowland known to its frequent visitors as "The Trough." Running through the valley is the river Hodder which eventually joins the Ribble, and the scenery is varied from wild moorland to parkland, forest, gentle valleys with mountain streams and quiet open spaces with views of craggy hills. Between Lancaster and Abbeystead there is a small observation tower with panoramic views. At Abbeystead is the Shepherd's Church with its beautiful stained glass windows depicting shepherds and their flocks. Pegs can still be seen in the porch where shepherds hung their crooks. Next to the church stands a public stable built by Thomas Townley in the 17th century.

The Trough of Bowland shows the north country at its best and at the county border the road passes between the peaks of Whins Brow (1,565 feet) and Fell Top (1,568 feet). The river Hodder and its tributaries, the Dunsop and the Langden Beck, meet at Dunsop Bridge which is a pleasant picnicking spot. Nearby is a trout farm where trout in all stages of growth are kept in tanks; they are used to restock rivers and are sold to angling clubs. Leedham's Garage at Dunsop Bridge runs a bus service from Clitheroe to Slaidburn via Bashall Eaves, Cow Ark, Whitewell, Dunsop Bridge, Newton and Slaidburn. There is no Sunday service, but parties of twenty will be taken if arrangements are made with the garage.

The hamlet of Whitewell, situated on the river Hodder, is renowned for its magnificent scenery. At St. Michael's church there is a notice telling visitors that part of the parish is in Lancashire and part in Yorkshire. The Whitewell to Chipping road winds in and out of the boundary between Lancashire and Yorkshire, and Browsholme Hall although on Yorkshire soil has a Lancashire address. At the village of Chipping the old school-house, dated 1684, and the ancient and interesting church of St. Bartholomew can be seen. The church was rebuilt in 1506 and restored in 1872; in the grounds are a Saxon holy water stoup and a sundial dated 1708. Parlick Pike, probably one of the best summits in Bowland, stands above Chipping and offers uninterrupted views of the Vale of Chipping, Bleasdale and the Fylde plain.

Holker Hall, Cark-in-Cartmel.

Route: From Lancaster, A590, to Grange on B5277, B5278. Opening Times: Daily except Friday, 10-30 a.m.-6 p.m. Admission: House. gardens and deer park, adults: $22\frac{1}{2}p$; children: $12\frac{1}{2}p$.

HOLKER HALL was built in the early 16th century and parts of the original structure form what is now called the Old Wing. This section is not open to the public as it is the home of Mr. Richard Cavendish, cousin of the present Duke of Devonshire, and he and his family live at Holker Hall all year round.

After an extensive fire in 1871 the 7th Duke of Devonshire repaired and extended the Hall, the rebuilding taking over three years to complete. Timber from the estate and local stone were used throughout, and it is this New Wing of the Hall which is open to the public from Easter to October. The wonderful workmanship of the interior woodcarving displayed in so many of the rooms is a well-known feature of the Hall, and the furniture, paintings and silver form a collection which traces back through many centuries of the Dukes of Devonshire.

The 22 acres of garden with its fountain, old-fashioned rose gardens and banks of flowers is also open to the public, and the Old Park Wood has recently been opened as a deer reserve. This extends from the Hall down to the shores of Morecambe Bay and contains one of the largest and oldest herds of fallow deer in England.

There are good car-park facilities and the Hall cafe, situated in the old coach house, is open for morning coffee, lunch, tea and snacks.

Leighton Hall, Carnforth.
Route: M6, A6 (Carnforth), to Yealand Conyers village. Opening Times: Wednesday, Sunday. Bank Holidays, May-September: 2-30 p.m. to 6-0 p.m. Admission: adults: 15p; children: 7½p.

THE first Leighton was a fortified manor house built by Adam d'Avranches on land granted to him in 1173 by William de Lancaster, Baron of Kendal. Ownership of the house and lands passed either by marriage or descent for six hundred years, and the names Crofts and Middleton appear regularly throughout this period. There are three other names which are interesting to notice: Adam de Redman, Adam de Yealand and Robert Conyers, since all three can be seen today forming the place names Yealand Redmayne and Yealand Conyers—two small villages in the immediate vicinity of Leighton Hall.

During the 1715 Rebellion the owner of Leighton, Albert Hodgson, was taken prisoner. The Hall was sacked and burned by Government troops and the lands were put up for auction in 1722, but were bought back for Hodgson by his friend Mr. Winkley. After his eventual release from prison, Hodgson returned to his ruined house. His daughter married George Townley and it was Townley money that financed the complete rebuilding of Leighton Hall, in the Adam style, and the replanting of the woods and park in 1763. Townley died without issue and the property was sold to Alexander Worswick in 1786; it was during his ownership that the house was refaced in the "new Gothick Style." In 1822 the property passed by sale to the Gillow family, famous for the furniture business of Gillow & Co., Lancaster. A later descendant, Richard Thomas Gillow, added the new wing to Leighton Hall in 1870. The present owner, Helen, is also of the Gillow family and is married to Mr. James R. Reynolds. They are permanently in residence at Leighton Hall.

The Hall is set in the most beautiful surroundings; the approach to the house is through open park land and the range of the Lakeland mountains lie behind the white limestone fronted Hall. A great many of the State Rooms are open to the public and contain some very fine examples of architecture, furnishings and paintings. As might be expected, Gillow furniture is much in evidence, being both of historical and family interest. The gardens, archery lawn and shrubbery walk are also open to visitors. One portion of the grounds contains a monument marking the site of the former family burial ground—a reminder of the times when Catholic families had difficulty in obtaining burial in consecrated ground. The old kitchens at the back of the house have been converted into refreshment rooms, and there are also free car park facilities. It might be helpful to bear in mind that, since Mr. and Mrs. Reynolds own several dogs visitors are requested not to bring their dogs into the Hall.

Cockersands Abbey.
Unclassified road off A588 South of Lancaster.

ALL that remains of this once great abbey is the 13th century chapter house with its fine vaulted roof. This building has been severley damaged by vandals in recent years and, in order to preserve it from further damage, arrangements have been made to have all openings built up so as to prevent access. More permanent restoration works will ultimately be carried out by the County Council and the Ministry of Public Buildings and Works.

Hawkshead Court House.
Half a mile north of Hawkshead at the junction of B5285 and the Ambleside-Newby Bridge road. Open: Daily except Mondays and Thursdays, from 2-5 p.m. Admission: 10p (children and students free).

The Courthouse dates from the 15th century and is all that remains of the manorial buildings of Hawkshead. It is thought that the Gate or Gatehouse was added in the 14th century to the older buildings. The building has crow-stepped gables and the walls are of rough rubble masonry, which is found on many barns in the Lake District. There is an arched passage leading into the present farmyard and on each side there are small rooms at ground level; it is possible that these were originally the guardroom and porter's lodge. The carved keystone on the arched passageway is a copy of the original, now in the farmhouse building. Above the keystone is a carving of a lion's head and over it is a niche, which held a figure of the Virgin Mary until 1843.

The courtroom measures approximately 14 yards by 7 yards, and was the venue for the manorial courts. In the south wall is a beautiful traceried window dated about 1410, while the east wall has a wide stone fireplace decorated with 13th century dog-tooth moulding. This suggested that the building existed before 1300 and was later remodelled, it is interesting to note that the Courthouse and the church are the only Pre-Reformation buildings in the parish. Crude limestone coffins have been found near the Courthouse and some inhabitants say that a "tall white robed female" haunts the lanes in the vicinity.

At one time the Courthouse was used as a loft and stables, and was in poor condition. Mr. S. Cowper, F.S.A., the late owner, undertook the repair and preservation of the building and provided new floors and doors, but apart from one new window the fabric of the building is unchanged. Mr. Cowper gave the property to the

National Trust in 1932, and the Ministry of Works have now scheduled it as an Ancient Monument. There is a folk museum at the Courthouse which houses a collection from the Abbot Hall Museum, Kendal.

Hawkshead Grammar School.
Route: From Coniston on B5285.

THE village of Hawkshead is well known to all who are familiar with the life of William Wordsworth, for it was here that he spent his early life. Hawkshead Grammar School was founded by Edwin Sandys, Archbishop of York, and the building dates back to 1675.

The young William Wordsworth came to the Grammar School in 1777 and remained there until 1783, during these six years he lodged at a nearby cottage which then belonged to Ann Tyson. The cottage is still there but is no longer open to the public, although most of the relics of Wordsworth's school days are kept at the school and exhibitions are held by arrangement with various organisations. There are no pupils at the old day school now, but it is possible to view the interior of the building after obtaining permission from the local authority.

The exterior of the building looks the same now as when Wordsworth knew it, with the coat of arms on the front, the sundial and the inscription recording the school's foundation in 1675.

Four years after leaving Hawkshead Grammar School, Wordsworth entered St. John's College, Cambridge. In the years that followed he must often have thought back to the days spent in the countryside around Hawkshead, and many of his poems make reference to the scenery that he had loved as a boy.

Hornby Castle, near Lancaster.
Route: Leave Lancaster on A683 (Ingleton road).

HORNBY CASTLE, now a private residence, is unfortunately not open to the public, but the grounds are occasionally opened on behalf of charity functions and village festivities.

Hornby stands on the river Wenning, a tributary of the Lune, and the castle's towering battlements dominate the landscape making the village a place well worth visiting. It is thought that Hornby was once the site of a villa belonging to some wealthy Roman; coins and a brick pavement have been found, and it lies on a direct line between Lancaster and the Roman camp at Barrow. At the time of the Norman Conquest, Hornby was held by Alric, a Saxon chieftain, and later passed by marriage to de Montbegon who came over from France with William's conquering army. The foundations of the castle were probably laid down by de Montbegon. The lands

The village of Wray, near Hornby.

and the castle were conveyed to Hubert de Burgh, who was Earl of
Kent and Lord Chancellor to King John; it was de Burgh who was
portrayed as one of the leading characters in Shakespeare's *King John*.
Hornby Castle subsequently came into the possession of the Neville
family about 1285 and the Harrington family in 1432, and later
became the home of Sir Edward Stanley who played a significant part
in the Battle of Flodden in 1514. This is commemorated in the stanza:

> *From Lancashire and Cheshire fast,*
> *They to the lusty Stanley drew:*
> *From Hornby whereas he in haste,*
> *Set forward with a comely crew, etc.*

Sir Edward Stanley was created Lord Monteagle and was also
made a Knight of the Garter in recognition of his services to the
Crown. Another Lord Monteagle, grandson of Sir Edward, was one
of those who discovered the Gunpowder Plot.

The majestic Castle of Hornby with its keep, turrets, battlements
and mullioned windows has seen its share of the blood, glory and
tragedy of a warlike past, but there is another aspect of Hornby as
seen through the eye of poet and painter. Turner must have spent
many hours in this locality as three of his well-known drawings show
"The Crook of Lune, leading to Hornby Castle," "Hornby from
Tatham Church" and "Ingleborough from Hornby Castle terrace."

Thomas Grey wrote in appreciation of the valley of the Lune and of the lands once part of Hornby Castle estates.

Lancaster Castle.
Open to the public from March to September, except when in use for Assize Court Sittings. Details may be obtained from the Court Keeper of the Castle.

A FORT may have stood on the site of the present Lancaster castle, overlooking the Lune estuary, as early as A.D. 90. The value of the site was not, however, realised until after the Conquest when almost the whole of Lancashire was given to Roger of Poitou. Here on the route between England and Scotland he constructed his castle, parts of which still remain.

The Shire Hall was built between 1796 and 1798. Around the walls there is a large number of javelins and a unique collection of coats-of-arms of Sovereigns, Constables of the Castle and High Sheriffs. These date back as far as the 12th century. The Crown Court, also built in 1798, was until 1835 the only Assize Court in Lancashire. The dock contains a branding iron and holdfast, where the unfortunate prisoner's hand was placed and branded for life with the letter M for malefactor. The last record of public branding was in 1811, but as late as 1826 prisoners were required to hold up their hands in Court to show the presence or absence of the letter M. The drop room, which was later the Grand Jury Room, is another part of the 1796-1798 building. Here prisoners were bound before being led out to their death by public execution, As many as 6,000 people would come on "Hanging Day," the last public execution being in 1865. The Keep was restored during the reign of Queen Elizabeth I, and the turret is called John o' Gaunt's Chair— it was in fact a beacon tower where fires were lit to warn of approaching invaders. Hadrian's Tower may well date back from Roman times, and now houses a small museum.

Lancaster Castle is still used as a prison and during the ages has housed criminals of all kinds. The old dungeons, where lunatic prisoners were once held, contain no light or ventilation except through a small iron grill above a three inches thick door. John Paslew, Abbot of Whalley, was executed here, and George Marsh was imprisoned in 1554 for heresy. Edmund Arrowsmith, a Catholic priest was executed at the castle, and George Fox, the founder of the Society of Quakers was imprisoned twice—in 1660 and 1663. Edmund Hartley was hanged here in 1597 for witchcraft, and the Pendle witches were either executed or died within these walls between 1612 and 1666. The staples which held them still exist in the Well Tower.

Levens Hall.

Route: M6, A6. Opening Times: Tuesday, Wednesday, Thursday, Sunday, 2 p.m.-5 p.m.; gardens open every day. Admission: house and gardens, 30p; garden only, 15p; steam exhibition, 10p. Children: half price. Special terms for large families: parties over 25 in number, 25p. Dogs allowed on leads in garden, but not in the house.

THE traveller making his way to Lancashire's north-westerly regions has to pass within a few miles of Levens Hall and, although officially it lies within the boundaries of Westmorland, it has therefore been decided to include the Hall in this book.

About 1170 a charter from William de Lancaster granted land at Levens to Norman de Hieland, a family associated with the district; later the name was contracted to "Yealand" and eventually the family became known as "de Redman." The de Redmans had strong connections with Lancashire as well as with Westmorland and Mathew de Redman (13th century), a soldier and member of Parliament for both counties, is thought to have built the first Levens Hall. The remains of its Pele Tower form the oldest portion of the present hall. De Redman descendants owned Levens Hall until 1562 when a Mathew de Redman sold the property to Sir Alan Bellingham. Even after the sale, Mathew's mother continued to occupy the hall and outlived Sir Alan. Thus it was not until 1580 that his son James Bellingham took up residence at Levens. He made many alterations and additions to the old house, inserting panelling and plaster-work and emblazoning the Bellingham coat of arms and his own initials at every available opportunity. The last Bellingham, Alan, was forced to sell as a result of placing the property in jeopardy through gambling, and by 1688 Col. James Graham had taken up residence. From that time onward Levens Hall passed either by marriage or descent, culminating in the present ownership by Robin Bagot.

The Hall has a remarkable collection of valuable paintings, silver and furniture including many pieces by the firm of Gillow of Lancaster. There are also a number of plucked instruments of the harpsichord type, one of which was made by the present owner, Mr. Bagot, in collaboration with Mr. Robert Davies.

The gardens at Levens are particularly noted for the topiary art, the work of Monsieur Beaumont who came from Versailles to lay out gardens for King James II, and who was later employed by Col. Graham. One tree is known to be over 800 years old and is called the Great Umbrella. The gardens are also remembered for a traditional festivity known as the Radish Feast which used to take place annually on 12th May. Sports were held and the people were served with radishes and bread and butter washed down with a potent Morocco beer brewed from a secret recipe. Any strangers were made to swallow a glass of this beer in one breath with the

Lancaster Castle.

Levens Hall and the topiary gardens.

toast "Luck to Levens whilst t'Kent flows."

For the mechanical antiquities' enthusiast, Levens has a unique collection of vintage monsters. This includes stationary industrial machines run from a modern boiler but showing the development of industrial power units. There are also steam locomotives of various classes, all lovingly cared for by the Bagot family and known by such names as "Annie" and "Bertha".

(See Ghosts of Levens Hall, p. 00).

Piel Castle, Piel Island, near Barrow-in-Furness.

Route: M6, A6, A590, A5087 (coast road) to Rampside and Roa Island. Boat to Piel Island.

PIEL ISLAND, originally named Fowdray, lies at the mouth of a natural harbour formed between the southern points of Walney Island and Foulney Island. The first castle was erected on this tiny island in the 12th century by the monks of Furness. Piel has been described as "a naked island of very few acres separated from the mainland by a narrow but dangerous channel" and as such it provided an ideal site for a fortified stronghold both for the protection of Piel Harbour and of the lands belonging to the monastery of Furness. The first structure probably consisted of a wooden tower standing on a mound and surrounded by a deep ditch with pallisades. Nothing of the original fortress can be seen, but in 1327 the monks decided to rebuild the castle on a much larger scale. It is the red sandstone ruins of the 14th century which now remain; the great keep or central tower, and the inner and outer baileys, together with the surrounding broad ditches and ramparted walls with towers.

In 1423 the Abbott of Furness was accused by the Crown Authorities of smuggling wool out of the country from "la Peele de Foddray"; an accusation which was probably well founded since Abbots of Furness derived much of their wealth from dubious sources. The next documented event in the history of Piel took place in 1487 when Lord Lovel and the Earl of Lincoln attempted to establish Lambert Simnel as true heir to the throne of England. In May of that year Lambert was crowned Edward VI in Dublin Cathedral; he and his supporters landed at Piel on June 4th and the harbour was filled with ships carrying over two thousand German mercenaries and a large number of Irish soldiers. Local tradition tells that they spent the night in Ulverston before marching through Yorkshire and onward to their defeat.

With the dissolution of Furness Abbey in 1537 Piel Castle, as part of the Abbey property, was taken over by Government troops. The Castle soon fell into disrepair, although the harbour remained in use until erosion of the southern side of the island and the altered course of the channel left Piel and its castle of no practical value. In the mid 19th century the Duke of Buccleuch had outworks constructed to protect the castle from further damage by the sea, and some restoration was carried out on the fabric itself. The castle is now maintained by the Barrow Corporation.

Piel Island has one other old building, the *Ship Inn*, which is still open to the public. There is a quaint old tradition connected with it known as the "Knighthood of Piel," which has been handed down over the centuries by the local fishermen. In one room at the inn is an ancient oak chair and anyone who sits in it must become a "Knight of Piel," the ceremonial knighting being performed by the King of the Island (the landlord). The "Knight" must pay for his "knighthood" by buying a round of drinks but he is assured that, should he ever be so unfortunate as to be shipwrecked on Piel Island, he may demand a night's lodging at the inn and as much as he can eat and drink.

Hill Top, Sawrey (National Trust).
Route: from Kendal, A591, B5284, car-ferry across Lake Windermere, B5285. Opening Times: Easter-October. Weekdays: 11 a.m.-5-30 p.m. Sundays: 2 p.m.-5-30 p.m. Admission: adults, 15p; children, 2½p.

HILL TOP was the home where Beatrix Potter wrote the well-known children's books, peopled with little animal characters whose adventures brought fame to their creator. In her earlier years, Beatrix Potter lived with her parents in London. It was a somewhat austere Victorian life which she found very confining to her artistic and imaginative nature. *The Tale of Peter Rabbit* came into existence as the result of a letter written to a small boy, describing the imaginary adventures of her own pet rabbit, the first black and white edition being published soon afterwards.

In 1896 the Potter family rented a large house in the village of Sawrey and spent the summer there, Beatrix explored the surrounding countryside with great delight for this area was a living example of the world her imagination had built. Some little while later Hill Top Farm was for sale. The royalties from *Peter Rabbit* made it possible for her to buy the property, at first as an investment, but gradually Beatrix extricated herself from the confining London family residence and made Hill Top her home. In the years that followed, her books show her love for the little farm at Sawrey, captured for all time in those beautifully detailed watercolour illustrations.

At the age of 47, Beatrix Potter became Mrs. William Heelis, wife of a country solicitor. Hill Top was not large enough for her husband and herself so they moved to Castle Cottage, but the little farm remained as her private work studio and sanctuary. After her marriage, Beatrix began to take a keen interest in the preservation of the Lake District for the nation and, with this aim in view, began buying property and land. She eventually left over 4,000 acres to the National Trust.

Her first little home, Hill Top, is National Trust property and is preserved almost exactly as she left it. Her furniture, notebooks, collection of French dolls and the various small objects which had formed the inspiration for her books for children are all still there—a quiet memorial to a remarkable woman.

Trees, Silverdale.

Route: M6, A6 (Carnforth). At the traffic lights at Carnforth turn left to Silverdale, and the garden is 5 minutes from the village. There is a bus from Lancaster. Opening times: The gardens are open daily from March 1st to August 31st except Mondays. Admission is free.

TREES, Silverdale, is a very popular garden, and visitors come here from a wide area. It is medium in size with limestone outcrops which have been planted with numerous alpines. There are large colourful herbaceous borders and a wide variety of shrubs, including Japanese Azaleas, although these are only one of the many different species to be seen.

Part of the garden is terraced and there are several lawns. The setting is particularly attractive; behind are the hills and down below the beach and sea shore at Silverdale. Although there is no charge for admission, there are collecting boxes in aid of the Retired District Nurses Fund and the National Trust Garden Scheme.

Churches

Aldingham: Church of St. Cuthbert.
On A5087 coast road from Ulverston.

THE first church here was probably Saxon, built as a memorial to St. Cuthbert. The pilgrims who carried his body rested here during their flight from the Danes, a legendary poem stating:

> *O'er northern mountain, marsh and moor,*
> *From sea to sea, from shore to shore,*
> *Seven years St. Cuthbert's corpse they bore.*

The oldest part of the present church is the 12th century southern arcade with short but massive pillars and rounded arches. The chancel is probably circa 1300 and contains traces of a Norman "Priests' Doorway" beneath the window in the south west corner, and a mysterious passage has recently been found in the east wall. Over the chancel arch are the royal arms. The font, now standing on a modern pedestal is undoubtedly very old, but the exact date is uncertain. A hagioscope or peep hole in the chancel wall is similar to that at St. Mary's, Urswick. The 14th century tower was built into the nave and is a mixture of architectural styles, and the bells— mentioned in 1553 as gifts of the parishioners—may have been brought from Furness Abbey or Cartmel Priory after the dissolution.

The original seat of the Lords of Aldingham is believed to be at Moat Hill, about half a mile south of the present village, where there is a legend of a submerged village. The earliest mention of Aldingham was in the Domesday survey of 1086 when Ernulf the Saxon held the land. About 1100 the Manor of Muchland was formed, the Lords weilding a great deal of power in the Middle Ages and earning many honours. Members of the family fought and were killed at Agincourt, Wakefield and Bosworth. They married well and in 1554 Lady Jane Grey, the nine days queen, was heiress of Muchland. After her execution on Tower Hill the manor reverted to the Crown and the gift of the living of the church to the Sovereign, Mary, which explains the royal arms on the chancel arch. In 1848 Queen Victoria also visited the church, and letters referring to her visit, written by her lady in waiting, are still in existence.

St. Cuthbert's Church, Aldingham.

Bolton-le-Sands: Church of St. Michael.
On A6 just South of Carnforth.

BOLTON-LE-SANDS church is one of the oldest in the district, and was known to have been in existence in 1094. At one time, together with the Priory Church at Lancaster, it was attached to the Abbey of St. Martin in Sees, Normandy, but in 1246 this right was relinquished in return for the church at Poulton-le-Fylde.

Although much of the church is of pre-Norman foundation, the base of the tower and the west doorway are all that remain from this period. Much of the tower with the pillars and arches date back to the 15th century; the roof probably contains the original oak. There are three bells, the oldest being about 15th century, the other two dated 1694 and 1724. On the north side of the sanctuary is a large stone slab bearing a beautifully carved inscription in old English and dated 1642. The nave has an interesting hammerbeamed roof. In the Baptistry at the foot of the tower are two interesting old stones. One consisting of a fragment of the ancient village cross covered with a bold interlacing pattern on the face and simple plait-work ornamentation on the edge. The other stone is a portion of a hog-back monument, on one side there is a roofing tile pattern and on the back traces of the outline of Thor, god of the Norsemen.

At the south end of the churchyard is the base of an Early English preaching cross; the shaft was found in the vicarage garden and the cross has now been restored as a memorial. Nearby is St. Michael's Well, where parish baptisms were carried out. Another well situated three quarters of a mile south-west of the village of Slyne, close to Townfield Lane, is dedicated to St. Patrick, and was supposed to have healing powers for sore eyes. Close by is a large flat stone called St. Patrick's Rest where the saint, after being shipwrecked off Heysham Head, is believed to have rested when passing through the parish to join the monks of Iona.

At Bolton-le-Sands there is a lane—where there was formerly a well —dedicated to St. Nicholas, patron saint of sailors and fishermen. Some years ago excavations were made in a field near this lane and the foundations of an ancient chantry were found, doubtless also dedicated to St. Nicholas. Prayers would have been said here daily for those who crossed the dangerous sands. As far back as the time of King John arrangements have been made for persons taking this route to be accompanied by an appointed guide. Although it is still possible to walk over the sands, it is strongly discouraged unless accompanied by an official guide. Occasionally large organised parties are arranged to cross the sands from Hest Bank—a distance of about 8 miles. For further information about the walk contact the Publicity Department at the Town Hall, Morecambe.

Cartmel Fell: Church of St. Anthony.
On an unclassified road between A5074 to Windermere and A590 to Grange-over-Sands.

THIS small church with its low mullioned windows and a tower with low saddle-back roof was built about 1504 and the floor slopes down to the altar owing to the natural fall in the ground. Perhaps one of the most interesting features is the stained glass in the windows, brought from Cartmel Priory in the 15th century. The old three-decker pulpit is a rare example and dates from 1698, and the large unusual pews are from early in the 16th century. Among other treasures in the church are a side table (used as an altar until 1936), rails, coffin stools and font dating back to 1712, and the Bishop's chair of 1645.

In the vestry is one of the rarest and most interesting relics, not only of the church but of all England. It is a figure of Our Lord, belonging to a large crucifix of the type originally found over the chancel screen; made of wood it has at some time been used as a poker. Near the entrance porch are marks where worshippers used to sharpen their arrows, and in the churchyard is a mounting block

Cartmel Priory Gatehouse.

with a post in the centre where horses could be tethered.

Cartmel Priory.
About 2 miles west of Grange-over-Sands.

THE priory was founded in 1188 by William Marshall, who ordained that "an altar should always be provided, with a priest, for the people of the town," thus ensuring the continuance of a church on the site. Constructed mainly in Transitional, Decorated and Perpendicular styles it has large and imposing proportions, the present walls being those built in monastic days. The central arches and those in the triforium have rounded heads, while some of the others are pointed.

After the Dissolution in 1537 the south aisle of the choir, known as the Town Choir, continued to serve as a parish church for 80 years. The rest of the priory fell into ruins, as did the other monastic buildings, the only one to survive being the "Gate House" (see below). In 1618 the church was re-roofed and the wonderful screen carved. Canopies were provided for the choir stalls and misericords, which had survived the years of neglect.

The archway of the north door with elaborate dog-toothed moulding should not be missed. The Piper Choir contains the only piece of original roof and has some exceptional misericords dating from 1450. The priory contains many treasures, including a very famous umbrella claimed to be 200 years old, a Vinegar Bible dating from 1716, and the first edition of Spenser's *Faerie Queene* printed in London in 1596.

Cartmel Priory Gatehouse.

THE gatehouse was probably built about 1330-40 as a fortified tower for Cartmel Priory. At the dissolution in 1537 orders were given for all the domestic buildings of the priory to be destroyed, those to escape being the Town Choir within the priory church and the gatehouse which was being used as a court house. From 1625-1790 it was in use as a school.

Now scheduled as an ancient monument and in the hands of the National Trust, the gatehouse contains a small museum and is used for exhibitions and meetings. Much restoration has been carried out, although a large part of the building is in its original state, and is remarkably well preserved. Visitors are able to see various rooms previously used as a guardroom and porters' lodge, together with the room above.

Halton Parish Church: St. Wilfreds.
Lies in the angle of M6 and A683, north of Lancaster.

THE earliest known church on this site was built in the 12th
century, although the present structure dates mainly from 1877.
Parts of the tower contain small amounts of Saxon and Norman
masonry, and it is believed it was rebuilt in the 14th century for
the present tower bears the date of 1597. In the churchyard are the
remains of three Anglican cross shafts dating from the 8th and 9th
centuries, and there is also the remains of a Norse cross dated
about 1,000 A.D. Built into the side of the hill is the fine two-tier
vault of the Bradshaw family.

Hawkshead: Church of St. Michael and All Angels.
On B5285 from Coniston.

THE church stands on elevated ground overlooking Esthwaite
Water. The present building which dates from 1350 incorporates
part of an earlier building of 1150. The pillars and arcading are unique
part of an earlier building of 1150. The pillars and arcading are
unique in the British Isles. Restorations have been carried out
in 1585 and again in 1633. The Sandys Chapel contains effigies of
William and Mary Sandys of Graythwaite Hall; their son, Edwin,
was the Archbishop of York from 1576 to 1589 and founded the
Hawkshead Grammar School, attended by Wordsworth.

To help the woollen industry, Parliament decreed in 1666 that all
burials must be in a woollen cloth, and a certificate issued. The
church has over 200 of these "Burial-in-Woollen" certificates, and
one may be seen by the north door. By the lectern is the oak register
chest, which was for the safe keeping of the parish registers and the
beginning of the modern system of registration. Outside, at the east
end of the church, is an ancient stone bench used as a general
meeting place for the hearing of sales and notices being cried after
Divine Service.

Heysham: Church of St. Peter.
B5273 from Lancaster.

IN beautiful surroundings on rising ground above Morecambe Bay
stands the church of St. Peter, the oldest portion being 10th
century Saxon. All that is left of this period is the west wall of the
nave, the stonework above the south arcade and the plain walling
above and around the chancel arch. The present chancel, with the
beautiful east and south windows, dates from about 1340. In the
15th century a south aisle was added, and the heavy gothic arches
inserted in the old wall. The rope pattern ornamentation on the
pillars is probably Saxon, and shows the dedication to St. Peter.

St. Peter's Church, Heysham.

On the west wall can be seen an unusual grave cover, probably of a crusader, with floriated cross of the 12th or 13th century. The belfry has a rare flat-topped cover. The hogbacked stone of Saxon origin is one of the more important and interesting antiquities of the church, being very rare and possibly the finest of its kind in existence. Near the churchyard gate is the shaft of a lovely early Christian 5th century cross.

Heysham: St. Patrick's Chapel.

ON the hill behind the parish church stands the small ruined chapel of St. Patrick. Measuring only 24 feet by 8 feet, it was roughly constructed of irregular sized stones held together with mortar of extraordinary strength, the walls being $2\frac{1}{2}$ feet thick. Only the east gable and part of the south wall remain.

The chapel was almost certainly built by the Celts in the 5th or 6th century. Unique to Heysham, and in fact to Great Britain, are the six stone coffins or graves carved out of solid rock in the form of a body. There are many legends of St. Patric, one being that he was the son of a member of the Roman garrison stationed at Dunbarton. At the age of fifteen, in 388 A.D., he was reputedly captured and taken as a slave to Ireland. Some years later he escaped and was shipwrecked in Morecambe Bay, coming ashore at Heysham where he rested and built the chapel before making his way back to Scotland.

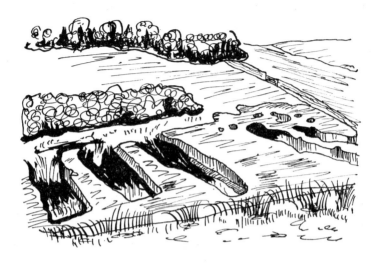

Saxon graves at St. Patrick's Chapel, Heysham.

Lancaster: The priory Church of St. Mary.

ALMOST from the beginning of Lancaster's history a church and a castle have stood on the hill overlooking the Lune estuary. Beneath the choir of the present church, built over 500 years ago, lie the remains of a Roman basilica, the exact position being marked by two sets of brass nails set in the floor. Part of the present west wall was built by the Saxons, and a Saxon doorway stands opposite the choir. One of the earliest crosses inscribed with Anglican runes was found in the churchyard and is now preserved at the British Museum: this indicates the presence of a church here in the 7th century.

When the church was being restored in 1911, a wall dating back to about 1180 was discovered and stones from this wall are still to be seen. The Transitional south-west doorway, dating from the same period, now forms the main entrance. It is evident that a large church stood here at the end of the 12th century, although practically nothing now remains, for everything but the west wall and the main doorway were removed to make way for the present church. The beautiful oak canopied Lancaster Choir Stalls, dating back to the 14th century, were originally used by the monks of St. Martin in the church which preceded the present one. In 1872, two stone coffins were unearthed during alterations, one being of a crusader and the other of a child. Both have been built into the vestry wall and can still be seen. A chalice and paten dating from

1631 form part of one of the finest collections of Communion Plate in the country.

In 1898 the plaster was removed from the west wall revealing a doorway dated about 1360, and in 1903 this was opened up to form an entrance to the tower which contains the brasses from the floor of the church. The most interesting is to the memory of Thomas Covell, Keeper at the Castle at the time of the trial of the Lancashire Witches. The present stone font was erected in 1848, but the Jacobean oak cover is dated 1631. An ancient octagonal font discovered in the vicarage garden can now be seen in the recess behind the Saxon doorway. It is difficult to date, but may be Saxon, making it one of the greatest treasures of the church.

Overton: Church of St. Helen.
Off the B5273 west of the Lune estuary.

BELIEVED to be perhaps one of the oldest church foundations in the county, St. Helen's dates back to Saxon times as is shown by the west wall of the church. Norman influence can be seen in the 12th century doorway on which the mouldings, although much eroded by the weather, can be clearly seen. The south nave wall and parts of the north nave wall are also Norman. The transept is unusual for it was built so that the congregation were unable to see the pulpit, which in 1772 was taken from its original place and built into the south nave wall. Excavations have recently proved that the original church had an apse at the east end; still to be seen are the old gallery and original timbered roof.

Tunstall: Church of St. John.
On A683 Lancaster to Kirkby Lonsdale road.

THE earliest record of Tunstall Church is in the Domesday Book, but the present building—the third on the site—is mostly 15th century and has been very little altered since that time. There are eight pillars on the north side, one of which has a design similar to that over the 14th century doorway in Thurland Castle. The Roman votive stone, now built into the side of the north-east window in the nave, probably came from the Roman camp at Barrow and was originally dedicated to Aesulepius, god of medicine and Hygeia, goddess of healing.

There is a broken 13th century sepulchral slab, originally 5 feet 6 inches long, now placed near the west door. The stone altar, bearing fine consecration crosses is probably Saxon, while the altar in the chapel dates from the 14th century and was taken from Thurland Castle. Also worthy of note are the beautiful stained glass windows of the 15th century, and the 16th century Bishop's Chair. The porch, which is two-storeyed, is probably one of the best pieces th century work in Northern Lancashire.

As "Brocklebridge Church," this building is mentioned in Charlotte Bronte's novel *Jane Eyre*.

Urswick: **Church of St. Mary.**
From Ulverston A5087, inland on to secondary road.

IN all probability Urswick was the first and original centre of Christianity in Furness. When Furness Abbey was built in 1127, deeds mentioned that St. Mary's was then about 250 years old. The fragment of a cross shaft with runic inscriptions and carvings now preserved within the church dates from the 10th century; a Viking wheelheaded cross is also preserved and is to be found on a glass-topped table at the back of the church. The massive squat tower is thought to be Norman, the upper part having been added later. It has a very small west door, above which are three niches where carvings once stood—unfortunately only one has survived.

To the left of the porch is a small mass hour dial of medieval origin—the dial is in good condition and should not be missed. The chancel is probably circa 1200 and, as at Aldingham, contains a 13th century hagioscope built into the wall. This allowed the congregation in the aisle to see the celebration of Communion. There is a simple three-deck pulpit, and most notable, excellent carved figures on the screen and organ case executed at the turn of the century by the Camden Guild of Carvers.

The small lancet window contains some stained glass taken from Furness Abbey, and in the east window can be seen the royal arms of Queen Mary who acquired lands in the area in 1554 (see also Aldingham). The church has two paintings executed about the middle of the 18th century by a local painter, James Cranke, the most notable being behind the altar and depicting the Last Supper. There are many other rare and unusual treasures to be seen. Within half a mile of Urswick village are the remains of an Iron Age settlement, and on Birkrigg Common a burial circle can be traced (see p. 47).

Warton, near Carnforth: **Church of St. Oswald.**
On an unclassified road off A6, north of Carnforth.

THIS beautiful church is set on rising ground surrounded by green fields and rocky crags. The south aisle is 14th century, probably marking the extent of the nave of an older medieval church. Rebuilding took place about 1480. The massive pillars on either side of the aisles are set at irregular intervals and support the slated roof which is continuous over the clerestoried nave and the chancel. Also dating from the 15th century are the south chapel, north and south aisles, south porch and western tower. The Chantry Chapel, which can be entered from outside by a small door, has the floor set below the main part of the building and was possibly left in its natural state during restoration.

The font, probably Norman, is lined with elaborate wrought iron lead work dated 1661, and bears the initials of the three vergers of that time. Robert Washington rebuilt the tower as a gift at the end of the 15th century; the family coat of arms can be seen on a shield —protected by glass—on the north side of the west window. The face of the tower clock is most unusual as it is bright red—it replaced the old clock which crashed to the ground when the roof gave way. The oldest bell dates from 1578. Archbishop Hutton, later of York, was a foundling of the parish, and in gratitude to the village he obtained the approval of Queen Elizabeth I to endow a school for boys and some almshouses. The deed given to the Archbishop and dated 1505 hangs on the wall of the vestry; also to be seen are the registers of baptism from 1568 written in a fine spidery hand on taut parchment.

On the 4th of July each year, in memory of the association of the church with the United States (see below), the Stars and Stripes are flown from the tower. Tradition has it that the flag shall be correctly folded when put away, the stars uppermost. Until recently a flag with 48 stars was flown, but this was noticed by a visiting American who arranged for the vicar to be sent a 50-star flag. A new flag is flown each day on the Capitol Building in Washington, and from the stock so acquired flags can be presented as needed. In July of each year there are visits of American choirs to the church— admission is free.

Nearby the **Old Rectory House,** dating from the middle of the 14th century, still retains the outer walls of the Great Hall and adjoining rooms. The immense gabled south wall, built of white stone and supported by a single buttress, stands to its original height. Inside, the old kitchens are dark and cheerless, with walls blackened by smoke from the large open fireplace. The upper rooms were probably a chapel and quarters where the surfs were housed, with only an open landing dividing them from the animals below. The building has been taken over by the Ministry of Works for preservation. Small groups may visit the Rectory without notice, but large parties wishing to have a conducted tour of the church and rectory should apply to the Rector one month in advance.

The Ancestry of the Washington Family. In about 1180 a family of noble birth went to County Durham to live in the small settlement of Wessington (now known as the mining village of Washington) and took the name of the town. By marrying into other noble families they acquired property over a large area, including a manor house at Helton Flechan in Westmorland in 1357. In 1363 a de Washynton, as the family were then known, married the widow of William de Lancastre and went to live at Levens Hall. It is at this time that the first mention is made of lands owned in Warton.

In 1483 Robert Washington was one of the wealthiest landowners in the county, mainly by inheritance, and it was he who had the tower of Warton parish church re-built. Robert married three times. The grandson of his elder son Robert, by his second wife, went to live in Northampton, having purchased Sulgrave Manor. It was here that the father of John Washington, who emigrated to America, lived until 1610. John became the great-grandfather of President George Washington, and Sulgrave Manor is now a place of pilgrimage for Americans visiting this country. Washingtons continued to live at Warton until 1823, the last being the Rev. Thomas Washington whose grave is in the churchyard. He was buried with his grandmother who died in 1751. The vicarage in which he lived and the Washington family house are still to be seen in the village.

6: Prehistoric and Roman Remains

THE area now known as Lancashire has been the home of men and women since before the dawn of recorded history. Flint implements dating from Mesolithic to Bronze Age times have been found on most of the high moorlands of Lancashire south of the Ribble. Such high ground is often a rewarding locale for the discovery of these Stone Age tools due to the fact that erosion of the overlying peat eventually uncovers the flints. Over 150 stone axe-heads of Neolithic date have been recorded from the county. In Langdale remains have been found of what have been called the Stone Axe Factories, where thousands of reject axeheads lie among the scree. It is thought likely that after being rough-cut the tools were sent elsewhere, probably to the coast where there was sandstone for grinding and polishing. Traces of Bronze Age man have also been found in various parts of Lancashire.

Remarkably little is known about the living customs of the various ancient peoples—they were often more voluble in death. The funerary rites of the Bronze Age People can be surmised because of their practice of interring the ashes of the dead in urns. Such finds were made at **Bleasdale,** near Garstang. Five miles west of Broughton-in-Furness lies **Swinside Stone Circle,** roughly 100 feet in diameter and comprising 50 stones many of which have fallen. This circle, referred to as "Sunkenkirk," is thought to be approximately 3,000 years old. Its exact purpose remains a mystery, but it is not difficult to imagine it as the site of sun worshipping or perhaps being similar to that of the Druid's Circle on the moors near **Turton** in the Bolton area. Another group of remarkable megaliths, the **Calder Stones** at **Liverpool,** show clear markings incised on their vast surfaces. Of particular interest is the spiral pattern which has been associated with ancient religions the world over and may be an early attempt to symbolise The Creation.

More comprehensive details of sites and earthworks can be obtained by purchasing the Ordnance Survey Map of Ancient Britain, or contacting the Lancashire Record Office, Preston.

The Banniside Urns.
Walna Scar road from Coniston to Duddon Valley.

ON the eastern slopes of Coniston Old Man lies Banniside moor.
At an elevation of 810 feet above sea level is a small area of
marshy ground near Boo Tarn and here traces of a stone circle some
70 feet across can still be identified. In 1909, W. G. Collingwood
excavated this site and slightly east of the centre of the circle found
an urn containing bone ash. A few feet away a second urn was uncovered and in addition to bone ash this urn also contained a pygmy
cup holding two human teeth which had belonged to a child of two
or three years old.

Perhaps the most interesting feature of the Banniside burial was
the discovery of a fragment of charred woollen fabric dating from
about 3,000 years ago—one of the earliest examples of woven fibre
known in England. Unfortunately this treasure soon disintegrated
when exposed to the air, but the Banniside Urns were put on
permanent display in the Ruskin Museum at Coniston.

Bleasdale Circle.
*Routes From Lancaster on A6. Turn at Garstang for Oakenclough;
signpost for Bleasdale.*

AT the beginning of this century a moorland burial spot dating
from the early Bronze Age was uncovered at Bleasdale. Here
enormous wooden posts were found which formed a prehistoric
burial circle over 3,000 years ago. To prevent the wood from
deteriorating the blocks were removed to the Harris Museum at
Preston where some of the timbers may be seen, and concrete posts
of a similar size were erected in their place. Further excavations
revealed the remains of two more circles, an outer ring approximately
150 feet in diameter of oak logs and a smaller ring of birch poles.
These were laid flat in the bottom of the ditch surrounding the inner
ring of oak posts. It was in the smaller ring that the eleven massive
oak posts were discovered near the point where the two outer circles
met. This innermost circle had an entrance flanked by two even
larger oak posts making it into the shape of a horseshoe. Within
this innermost circle of horseshoe form, two funeral or cinerary
urns containing human ashes and bones were uncovered. These urns
were also removed to the Harris Museum. Bleasdale Circle is an
example of a "palisaded barrow" and the innermost circle of posts
probably represents a "house of the dead". Parallels for these
palisaded barrows can be found in Holland and North Germany.
The fact that the original wooden posts still exist make it unique.
The ring of concrete posts marking the burial circle stand in a lonely
and desolate spot in the heart of the Bleasdale fells; the setting is
most impressive and it is easy to imagine primitive man worshipping
here.

Pennington Village.
Routes South of Ulverston on A590.

THE village of Pennington lies two miles south of Ulverston, and its church, though rebuilt in comparatively modern times, incorporates much of the history of the area. A Norman tympanum, once part of the entrance arch but now set into the wall, bears the runic inscription which in translation means: "Gamel founded this church, Hubert the mason wrought." Gamel de Pennington, who took his name from the village, also founded Conishead Priory in the 13th century. The stone-post remains of the village stocks and a sundial dated 1680 are also to be found near the church.

Beyond the village lies Castle Hill which is the site of a Saxon fortress, while close by are two ancient tumuli known as "Ella" and "Conynger" Barrows. An ancient legend tells that the Lord Ella lies sleeping here with his golden sword at his side, and indeed when Conynger Barrow (King's Mound) was excavated a sword was found alongside some fragments of human bone! It is always satisfying when legend is substantiated by objective evidence, and one wonders if there is also some truth in the legend of Great Urswick, an ancient site several miles south-east of Pennington. Urswick Tarn is now a flat expanse of water, but it is said that a vanished city lies beneath the mere. Perhaps the lake dwellers of Prehistoric times did in fact build a "village on stilts," and all that now remains is a vague memory handed down by word of mouth.

Birkrigg Circle.
Routes From Ulverston A5087; turn inland on to secondary road.

EXCAVATIONS in the Barrow peninsula have produced considerable evidence of Neolithic and late Bronze Age culture, over 60 barrows, cairns and burial circles having been found in this general area. One such site is on Birkrigg Common beyond Urswick, and though locally known as the Druid's Temple it has almost certainly no connection with the Druids.

Urswick Stone Walls.

WHEN excavated the stone walls at Urswick were found to be the remains of a pre-Roman communal settlement of a much later date, consisting of two large enclosures—one oval and one quadrangular—three walls measuring 180 feet and a fourth wall of 150 feet. The oval enclosure is roughly 320 feet long and 250 feet wide and is thought to be the earlier of the two, the date of construction having been estimated as between 2,060 and 2,160 years ago. This oval camp encloses a series of irregular curved walls built of limestone slabs with an infilling of smaller blocks; in the centre lie the remains of a large hut and several smaller huts which possibly belonged to a chieftain and his followers. The quadrangular enclosure is probably of a later date and may owe its shape to the Roman influences, being a crude copy of the plan of Roman encampments. Finds at Urswick Stone Walls and at the nearby fortified camp of Skelmore Heads suggest that both these settlements date from the period immediately prior to, and succeeding, the Roman invasion.

Roman Lancashire.

THERE is abundant evidence of the Roman occupation of Lancashire, including coins and pottery, the remains of earthworks and burial sites, and part of an original Roman road on Blackstone Edge. Here the cobblestone road can still be seen, with a deep groove running down the centre. The Romans built two major roads through the county, the principal one running from Manchester to Carlisle and the other from the Cheshire salt towns across the Mersey at Warrington to Lancaster. On these two roads were constructed the Roman forts at Wigan, Manchester, Lancaster, Ribchester and Overborough. Morecambe Bay, which was then called Moricambe Sinus, was used as an anchoring place for their ships.

The largest number of Roman remains have been discovered at Ribchester, where parts of the original fort may still be seen. A Roman altar found at Wigan is now built into a wall of the church tower. Several Roman remains have also been found at Lancaster, Manchester and Overborough.

Hadrian's Tower at Lancaster Castle is thought to have been part of the Roman fort built on this site, and it is believed that the tower housed a horse-mill in Roman times. Beneath the choir of the nearby Priory Church of St. Mary are the remains of a Roman basilica, the exact position marked in the wooden floor by two sets of brass nails. Many of the Roman relics discovered in this part of the county may be seen in the Lancaster Museum, and include inscribed stones, milestones, altars, pottery, coins and some tiles discovered at the site of a Roman tilery in 1774. In 1794, during the construction of the Preston to Lancaster canal, a group of sculptured stones was unearthed at Ashton and they are thought to be unique in this country.

Roman coins have been discovered in Furness and at Castlehead near Grange-over-Sands. The rectangular stone wall enclosures at Urswick are thought to have been based on a Roman prototype, and can still be seen.

Public Library and Museum, Ramsden Square, Barrow-in-Furness.
Open: As for the Library.

THE Museum is housed with the library and although small has some interesting exhibits. Local pre-historic finds from the Stone Age to the Iron Age are on display together with a collection of Lake District bygones. Of particular interest to boys of all ages is the loan collection of ships model from Vickers, the famous shipbuilding firm.

Steam town, Warton Road, Carnforth.
Open daily, 9 a.m. to 5 p.m. Admission: Adults 10p. Children under 12 accompanied by an adult, FREE. Car park. Refreshments. Shop. Gala days, admission 40p., (extension until 7 p.m.). Children as above.

STEAMTOWN is a live steam museum, which is fast becoming one of the foremost in the country with an impressive array of rolling stock. This includes a French Railways SNCF Pacific locomotive which prior to its withdrawal in 1968 hauled the famous Fleche D'Or (Golden Arrow) express between Calais and Paris. Also in the Museum is an ex L.M.S. Ivatt class 2 2-6-0 No. 6441 restored to a Midland Railway maroon livery. There are five ex L.M.S. Stanier class 4-6-0s: 44871 painted B.R. lined black livery; 44932 in blue; 45407 in Furness red; 45231 in L.M.S. black; and 44767 in L.M.S. black and red post-war livery. This last is a unique engine as it is the only one of the class fitted with Stephenson link motion.

Other engines are: ex LNER B1 class 4-6-0 No. 61306 in apple green livery; ex Eastern Gas Board 0-4-0 vertical boiler shunting locomotive known as "Gasbag"!; SNCF K class 4-6-2 No. 231 K 22 built in 1914; two ex LMS 2-6-4Ts Nos. 2073 and 2085 restored in LNWR and Caledonian liveries respectively; Peckett 0-4-0ST "Caliban"; a Shell rail tanker.

Gala days are held at Steamtown on Sundays from the beginning of February at about five-week intervals, and engines are steamed and footplate rides are provided. During 1971 it is hoped to acquire

Locomotive at Steamtown, Carnforth.

a German locomotive and several industrial engines. Negotiations are also progressing for the use of a $3\frac{1}{2}$-mile stretch of line from Lakeside to Haverthwaite and some of the locomotives housed at Carnforth are destined for this project. Gala days in 1971 will be Whit Monday, May 24th; June 27th; July 25th; August 29th and August 30th (Bank Holiday Monday); September 26th; and October 31st.

Brantwood, East Lakeside, Coniston.
Route: B5285 from Coniston to Hawkshead, turn after 1 mile for East Lakeside. Admission: $12\frac{1}{2}p$; children, $7\frac{1}{2}p$. Free car park. Opening times: February—November, Weekdays and Sundays, 10 a.m. to 5-30 p.m. Saturdays, 2 p.m. to 5-30 p.m.

BRANTWOOD will make an ideal day out for people of all ages and interests (set on the edge of Coniston Water in the heart of beautiful countryside.)

For many years until his death in 1900, Brantwood was the home of John Ruskin, writer, artist and social reformer. It was here that he retired from his position of Professor of Art at Oxford University. Brantwood is now preserved as a museum, and shows Ruskin's paintings, relics and furniture, over 200 of his original pictures and a large collection of work by other artists including Turner, Prout,

Fairfax Murray, Laurence and Hunt. There is a display of Ruskin's books, sketches and specimens, while his coach and boat are still kept in the boat house.

Brantwood lies in its own Nature Reserve which covers a mile of the lake shore and stretches to the fells behind the house and the border of the Grizedale Forest. The lake setting, with the Coniston Fells rising to over 2,500 feet, make views almost unequalled in beauty, interest and appeal. The Nature Reserve has a marked nature trail and is magnificent walking country.

The John Ruskin Museum, Coniston.
The Museum is open from Easter to October. Times of opening are 10 a.m. to dusk. Admission is 2½p.

THE John Ruskin Museum was opened in August 1901. Throughout the 1880s various plans had been discussed to enlarge the Institute in Yewdale Road and build a new museum. Ruskin, who was then living at Brantwood, laid the foundation of the present collection in 1884 with the presentation of 124 mineral specimens, and two years later a similar collection of fossils and minerals was donated by Dr. Kendall and Mr. John Bell. These collections were then displayed in the assembly room of the Institute. In 1895 W. G. Collingwood, Ruskin's secretary and biographer, became interested in the plans for the museum at Coniston, and with his help enough money was raised for work to begin on extensions to the existing building. During the years that followed Collingwood arranged several exhibitions of Ruskin's books, manuscripts and drawings to raise money for the museum building fund.

In 1901, a year after Ruskin's death, the new museum was officially opened. W. G. Collingwood presented many interesting items, including the Banniside Urns (see page 46). The Severn family, who had been related to Ruskin and were then living at Brantwood, donated many exhibits from his former home. The museum now houses a collection of original works by Ruskin, reproductions of engravings which were made to illustrate his books, and other items which help to provide a fascinating picture of his life.

Lancaster City Museum, Market Square, Lancaster.
Open daily Monday to Saturday, 10 a.m. to 5.30 p.m. Closed Sunday, and official holidays.

THE City Museum is housed in the Old Town Hall. The entrance hall contains a selection of paintings depicting ancient Lancaster, while a small gallery is used for exhibitions and displays. Off the main corridor is a room displaying neolithic axe heads and Bronze Age weapons, many of the items having been presented to the museum by H. S. Cowper of Hawkshead. There is also a collection of Roman inscribed stones discovered in and around Lancaster, which include part of a sandstone dedication slab found at St. Mary's Church, Lancaster in 1863, a cylindrical milestone located near Caton in 1803, and a sandstone altar brought to light in the church-yard at Halton in 1794.

In 1588 Lancaster received a set of troy weights and avoirdupois weights issued by the Crown, these and various capacity measures forming one of the best provincial collections of weights and measures. The Museum received a large collection of porcelain ivory and jade in 1945, and there is also a collection of furniture by Gillows of Lancaster—one of the leading cabinet makers of the 18th century. There are also a number of clocks on display, Lancaster being at one time a centre for clock makers.

The City Museum incorporates the Museum of The King's Own Royal Regiment (Lancaster), which includes various items of uniform and equipment dating from the 18th century onwards. Of particular interest is a uniform belonging to Captain Thomas Plumbe of the Royal Lancashire Militia Regiment; this dates from the period 1759/1765.

8:

Nature Reserves and Bird Sanctuaries

FOR readers who are interested in nature reserves and the preservation of all types of wild life, details of as many reserves as possible have been included. The wardens and those in charge stress the necessity for extreme care when visiting the reserves, and ask for the help of visitors in preserving the many rare and valuable species that may be seen.

Cleveleymere Nature Reserve, Forton.
Just off A6, north of Garstang.

THE old gravel workings by the river Wyre at Forton comprise some 46 acres and have become very attractive to winter migrants. Part of the reserve area is flooded while a marshy field with scrub and small pools provides a useful series of habitats for breeding species. The Reserve is owned jointly by the Lancashire Naturalists' Trust Ltd. and the Cleveleymere Fly Fishers, and access is strictly limited. All enquiries should be made to the Hon. Warden, S. Craig, Esq., 18, Beechwood Avenue, Fulwood, Preston. The reserve may be viewed from the road with field glasses, but the public are requested not to enter without prior permission.

Barnaby's Sands Nature Reserve, Preesall.
Off A588 road to Preesall.

BARNABY'S SANDS consists of a complex of 142 acres of ungrazed salt marsh, shingle banks and heath on the north bank of the river Wyre near Knott End. The rich mixed marsh vegetation containing an abundance of Sea Lavender (Limonium spp.) is a particularly unusual feature of a west coast salt marsh and is of special scientific interest. The masses of purple flowers to be seen at the end of July are also very attractive, but they should not be picked. (See over for details of access).

Burrows Marsh Nature Reserve, Stalmine.

BURROWS MARSH is similar to Barnaby's Sands and is situated only a little further upstream on the north bank of the river Wyre. It has a much better representation of the transitional zones between saline and freshwater conditions, these zones being particularly interesting as they are only occasionally found on west coast marsh systems.

Access to both these reserves is from Burrows Lane. Further enquiries should be addressed to E. F. Greenwood, Esq., Hon. Sec., Lancashire Naturalists' Trust Ltd. (Central Region), 35, Chapman Road, Fullwood, Preston, Lancs. PR2. 4NX.

Leighton Moss Reserve, Silverdale, Carnforth.
Unclassified road N.N.W. of Carnforth.

LEIGHTON MOSS reserve covers 200 acres of reedbeds, and has great numbers of migratory and nesting birds including some rare species. Those that can be seen include bitterns, reed warblers, water rail, mallard, teal, shoveler, pochard, tufted duck, gargeny and a few spotted crake. Lapwing, redshank and snipe are abundant. Birds passing on their way to breeding and wintering grounds include reed buntings, sedge warblers and the rarer grasshopper warbler and the lesser whitethroat. Otters can be seen fishing in the mere, while red deer, foxes, badgers, red squirrels, weasles, stoats, shrews and voles are also to be found. The Moss has many butterflies and 266 species of moth.

Visitors are welcome on the public footpath, and application for use of the public hide should be made to the Warden. Access to other parts of the reserve is by permit only, obtainable from Royal Society for the Protection of Birds, The Lodge, Sandy, Beds.

Roundsea Wood Nature Reserve.

THE primary interest of Roundsea is the variety of habitats with their rich flora and fauna, together with many different types of vegetation forming a unique area in a small space. Sessile oakwood, ashwood and yew-wood on limestone and slate, raised bog mixed fen and west coast saltmarsh are all to be seen. A permit is required to visit the Reserve and may be obtained from the Regional Officer, Merlewood Research Station, Grange-over-Sands.

Rusland Moss Nature Reserve.
Rusland is on an unclassified road North of Newby Bridge.

THIS Reserve is part of a raised bog only 20 feet above sea level; it originated from a shallow lake and is one of the few remaining examples in the southern Lake District of a moss that has not been damaged beyond repair. Although partially cut and drained, the moss still retains most of the characteristic bog plants and animals. A permit is required to visit the Reserve and may be obtained from The Regional Officer, Merlewood Research Station, Grange-over-Sands.

South Walney Nature Reserve, Walney Island.
Route: A590 into Barrow, and across connecting bridge. The Reserve is open all year round (see section on permits).

WALNEY ISLAND is eleven miles long, but it is the two miles at the southernmost tip which have been protected as a nature reserve. The location contains a varied terrain—mud flats, sand and pebble beaches, sand dunes, bracken areas and fresh water pools—and thus a wide variety of resident and migratory birds as well as many small vertebrates are observable in their natural habitat. Off shore several types of dolphin and of seal are frequently sighted, and even the "Killer Whale" has been noted on several occasions.

The mixed breeding colony is shared by many types of sea bird. Chief among these are the herring gull and the black backed gull, the estimated population of each species being 17,000 pairs. In the breeding season the ground is the domain of the male birds, each one raucously proclaiming and defending the invisible boundaries of his territory. Overhead the female birds wheel and turn, select their intended mate, and descend to his territory to "beg" for the acceptance response—a regurgitated fish. The innate rituals of courtship and pairing and the subsequent responsibilities of chick rearing are unfailingly carried out by each succeeding generation. The language of calls and of response stimuli are so clearly defined that they become obvious to the patient human observer. To the ornithologist and layman alike it is a wonderful experience to be able to witness these spectacles of nature.

Hides have been provided in suitable positions and are available to visitors on application to the Resident Warden. If it is intended to take photographs this fact should be mentioned at the time of application.

Trapping and Ringing: Three Heligoland traps are situated on the Reserve and all rings provided; use of these facilities is strictly limited to those holding a N.E.R.C. Licence.

Permit details: The Reserve is open all the year round and visitors are welcome. A permit is required and can be obtained on application to the Hon. Sec. A charge is made of: 25p, April to September; 15p, October to March. Children under seven years are admitted free; children of seven to fifteen years are charged 5p.

Accommodation: For visitors wishing to stay on the Reserve there are cottages available—self-contained with mains water,

Calor Gas lighting and cooking. They cost 35p per person per night or £2.50 per person per week. Bookings can be made for any period and should be addressed to Jas. H. Mitchell, 82 Plymouth Street, Walney Island, Barrow-in-Furness.

Wyre/Lune Bird Sanctuary.

THE Sanctuary has been established in the intertidal area between the Rivers Wyre and Lune, including Preesall, Pilling and Cockerham Sands. The purpose of the Sanctuary is to afford protection to the winter goose roost. Pink-footed and Grey Lag Geese are the most common species occurring in the area with smaller numbers of Whitefronted, Bean and Barnacle Geese. Further information may be obtained from the Nature Conservancy, Merlewood Research Station, Grange-over-Sands.

Nature Trails.

THE trails and walks are easily accessible, each trail having its own leaflet showing the route and points of interest on the way.

Claife Walk: From the Ferry on Windermere. Run by the National Trust and Freshwater Biological Association. The leaflet, price 5p, is available from the F.B.A., Ferry House, Windermere.

Eaves Wood, Silverdale: Arranged by the National Trust and the Lancashire Naturalists' Trust. Guides are obtainable from Mrs. Jones-Parry, 27, Spring Bank, Silverdale, via Carnforth, price 5p. The National Trust Area Office, Borrans Road, Ambleside, will also supply information on the above trails.

Riding Wood: Arranged by the Forestry Commission, Grizedale. Guide 7½p from Grizedale. Shows some of the work mentioned under "Grizedale Wild Life Centre." (See below).

Grizedale Forest Wildlife Centre.
On unclassified road about 3miles south of Hawkshead.

FACILITIES for the visitor to Grizedale Forest, now owned by the Forestry Commission, include a deer museum and wild life centre, an arboretum and tree nursery, a watchtower called "Treetops" and "photo-safari" high seats. Provision has also been made for camping, on a ground run by the Camping Club of Great Britain, and there are several car parks. At Coniston Water there are short forest walks, picnic areas and lay-bys.

Treetops Observation Tower: Treetops has been built by the Forestry Commission to enable members of the public to study and photograph the wild life of the forest. The tower is twenty feet high and the cabin is reached by a rung ladder. Both red deer and roe deer are to be found beneath the larches which surround the tower, while some twenty to thirty species of birds can be seen regularly and many others are occasional visitors. The nearby tarn is a haven for wildfowl; foxes, badgers and hares also inhabit this area as well as a complex of smaller mammals and insect life. As most movement in the forest takes place in the early morning and late evening, book either for a morning or evening watch. Parties should be in the tower at least half an hour before dawn or two hours before dusk, and must be prepared to sit still and quietly for periods of two or three hours. It is advisable to bring a pen and a torch to record observations. The tower holds a maximum of 10 people and a charge of 20p per person with a minimum of £1 is made for each watch. Bookings should be made in advance through the Head Forester, Grizedale, Hawkshead, Ambleside, Westmorland (telephone: Satterthwaite 214), from whom further information is also available.

Photo-Safari in Lakeland: Grizedale is the first forest in Great Britain to offer the facilities of a Photo-Safari, which is a wild life service developed by the Forestry Commission specifically to serve the photographer. With the use of "high seats" the cameraman can overcome the natural alertness of wild creatures and photograph the animals which can also be seen from "Treetops." It must be emphasized that this service is essentially designed for the reasonably equipped amateur and professional and is not for the box camera enthusiast! The ten hides, which are fully enclosed and provide full protection from the weather, are available for use by clubs or individuals. The fee per photographer is £5.25 per week or £1 per day which includes all facilities. It includes Juniper Tarn—the wild fowl rearing tarn where opportunities to photograph the Greylag Geese and other wildfowl are available. All bookings must be made through the Head Forester (see above). The greatest care must be exercised at all times by people using these photographic facilities and those of "Treetops" to ensure that no risks whatever are taken with regard to fire. Stoves are not allowed and extreme care must be observed at all times when smoking.

Grizedale Angling Club: Through a lease from the Forestry Commission, the Club controls the fishing of Grizedale beck which runs through the forest. The beck carries a good stock of brown trout and has a late migratory run of sea trout. Visitors may fish in this water by permit sold at a reasonable fee at the Camp Shop.

9:   Docks and Watersways

The Port of Barrow-in-Furness.

THE port of Barrow is situated in the south-west of Furness, and has an outer deep water harbour and the Ramsden Dock Basin. The largest commodity now imported into the docks is woodpulp from Scandinavia, while from the same area comes iron and scrap ingot moulds. Exported are firebricks, fireclay and other building materials to Norway, and cargoes of machinery from Vickers Ltd. to all parts of the world. Now that the import of ore for the nearby ironworks has ceased, Barrow does not carry the traffic of former times, although boats with a draught of up to 30 feet can be accommodated in the harbour. A tour of the docks can be arranged by applying in writing to the Dock Manager, Dock Office, Ramsden Dock Road, Barrow-in-Furness.

Canal Cruising.

THE Lancaster Canal, which originally ran between Kendal and Wigan, was opened in June, 1819. It was planned to be carried over the Ribble estuary at Preston on a massive aqueduct, but the cost of this proved to be prohibitive and the two sections were joined by a tramway. In 1879 the tramway was closed; the canal was thus left in two halves and the southern portion fell into disuse. On the Kendal to Preston section a daily passenger service was started in 1820, covering the 57 miles in 14 hours, and in 1833 an express boat was introduced which cut this time to $7\frac{1}{2}$ hours. The passenger boats were finally withdrawn in 1849. The Lancaster Canal now runs from Preston to Tewitfields north of Carnforth, a distance of 42 miles, with a branch off to Glasson Dock, about $3\frac{1}{2}$ miles, with six locks.
Almost the whole length of the canal runs through beautiful countryside, skirting the Pennine hills and on through tree-bordered banks, northwards across the River Lune over the famous John Rennies aqueduct bridge to Hest Bank and the foothills of Westmorland. There are no locks on this section. The Port of Glasson Dock is well worth a visit with its Yacht Basin and Sea Dock.

Today the boats on the Lancaster Canal are used solely for pleasure purposes; many are privately owned but there are a number of passenger cruisers. *The Lady Fiona* has a 3½-hour cruise from Lancaster on Tuesdays, Wednesdays, Thursdays and Sundays from Easter until the end of September, commencing at 2 p.m. from the British Waterways Wharf, Aldcliffe Road, Lancaster. Charges are: Adults 30p; children 17½p. Refreshments are served on board; private parties are also catered for. For further information apply to Mr. D. C. Fox, 1, Woodland Avenue, Thornton, Blackpool, FY5. 4HA.

Nor'West Holiday Cruisers hire out boats by the day or week accommodating up to six persons for £5 per day and vessels for up to 11 persons for £7.50. Weekly charges vary according to the size of the boat and the season; from March to October they are from £15 to £50. Further details may be obtained by writing to Nor'West Holiday Cruisers, Canal Wharf, Galgate, nr. Lancaster.

The Lancaster Canal Trust is an organisation which, while engaged on projects to improve the canal, also organises private cruises of the canal for its members. Membership of the Trust is 50p for adults; 25p for juniors; 75p for family membership. Further details may be obtained by writing to the Public Relations Officer, 16, Cranbourne Avenue, Church, Accrington.

Sports and Hobbies

IN this section it has only been possible to give the names and addresses of a few of the more specialised clubs. Those requiring information on other clubs and societies in local areas should apply to their Town Hall or Public Library where a comprehensive list will be found.

Angling

IT is usually possible to obtain day tickets to fish from the many piers that abound on the Lancashire coast line. For those who prefer a more specialised type of angling it is often possible to obtain day tickets or weekly permits to fish in one of the rivers or reservoirs. As the names and addresses of local secretaries are liable to change, those interested should obtain a complete and up to date list from the Lancashire River Authority, 48 West Cliff, Preston, telephone number Preston 54921.

Archery.

ORIGINALLY a means of hunting and war, archery has been considered a sport for many hundreds of years. The Royal Company of Archers was founded in 1676. In Lancashire there are many archery clubs both for field and target archery, the oldest club dating back to 1902. This is the Bowmen of Pendle and Samlesbury who shoot in the grounds of Samlesbury Hall. Other clubs include the Blackpool Bowmen, Billinge Bowmen (near Wigan), the Bowmen of Overdale, the Grange and Allithwaite Archers, Mersey Bowmen, Preston Archers and the Walverden Bowmen. Further information may be obtained by writing to the Secretary of the Grand National Archery Society, 20, Broomfield Road, Chelmsford, Essex.

Canoeing.

THERE are a number of local canoe clubs in Lancashire affiliated to the British Canoe Union, these including the Manchester Canoe Club, the Grappenhall Athletic Canoe Club, the Lakeland

Canoe Club and the Canoe Camping Club. Membership of the B.C.U. is 75p per year for a full member, and further details may be obtained from the General Secretary, British Canoe Union, 26/29 Park Crescent, London, W.1. The canoe clubs in Lancashire arrange many events, both inside and outside the county, and these include slaloms, sea surfing, cruises, regattas and wild water races. Meetings are held on stretches of the Dee, Lune, Ribble, Wharfe and other Pennine rivers.

Folk Dancing.

THE English Folk Dance and Song Society (North Lancashire District) both organise and take part in many interesting events throughout the county. These include barn dances, folk dance parties and social events during the winter months, and displays at carnivals and processions during the summer. The Leyland Morris Men undertake evening tours of the local towns and villages, sometimes accompanied by the Furness Morris Men and the Hoghton Rapper Sword Team. The Manchester Morris Men specialise in the traditional clog processional dances of this region. Further details of the many local clubs and events may be obtained by writing to the Area Organiser, 4 Bluecoat Chambers, School Lane, Liverpool 1.

British Gliding Association.

LANCASHIRE has two gliding clubs, and newcomers to this sport may go along any Saturday or Sunday and introduce themselves. If under 21 they will have to have their parents' written permission before the club will take them up on an air experience flight. Holiday courses are run by the Lakes Gliding Club at Walney Island from June to August and cost about £26—this includes bunkhouse accommodation, all meals and approximately 20 flights. Families, providing the children are over the age of 16, are accepted, and bookings are weekly from Friday to Saturday. The addresses of the two Lancashire Clubs are: The Blackpool and Fylde Gliding Club, Blackpool Airport, Blackpool. Telephone: 41526. Lakes Gliding Club, Walney Airfield, Barrow-in-Furness. Telephone 41458.

Go-karting.

THE Lancashire Kart Club organise monthly meetings at Burton-wood, near Warrington, throughout the year. Membership of the club is £1.50 per year, and for juniors 75p. The club is R.A.C. approved, and members can compete at any R.A.C. circuit in the U.K. or in any international event held abroad. Other clubs in

Lancashire include the Ribble Kart Club which meets at Flookburgh (near Grange-over-Sands); the Morecambe and Heysham Kart Club which meets at Heysham Head; and the Lion Kart Club which organises events at Tern Hill.

Pony Trekking.

FOR those interested in pony trekking and riding holidays the following stables were registered under the Riding Establishments Act, 1964. In all cases suitable clothing should be worn and some previous knowledge of riding should have been obtained.

Hawkshead: Tarn Hows Hotel, Hawkshead, Ambleside, telephone Hawkshead 330. 5-day residential riding holidays. Prior booking required the day before (longer notice in the holiday season) with details of weight and height.

Sawrey: Captain C. G. Dand, Sawrey Knotts Hotel and Stables, Far Sawrey, Ambleside, telephone Windermere 2105. Residential riding holidays, and half-day, full day and weekly treks. All rides accompanied.

Windermere: Mrs. J. E. Allchin, Limefit Park, Windermere, telephone Ambleside 2300. Half- and full-day treks; minimum age 10 years. Six-day holidays from July to September, and special arrangements for school groups. All rides accompanied.

Miss M. Jagger, Craig Level Riding School, Windermere, telephone 3481/3572. Trekking from April to September daily, with special treks for children. Prior booking necessary; accommodation arranged nearby if required.

Sub Aqua Clubs.

THE British Sub Aqua Club has many local branches throughout Lancashire, the addresses of which can be obtained from the headquarters of the club at 25 Orchard Road, Kingston-upon-Thames, Surrey. Inland as well as coastal towns are represented and, although most of the diving is done in the sea and lakes, many clubs have "practice nights" at their local swimming baths. Included among the activities of sub aqua enthusiasts are such programmes as: (a) underwater surveys for different biological, archaeological and fishing societies; (b) searches for sunken boats and wrecks; (c) lobster and crab fishing. Organised parties of B.S.A.C. members travel to diving locations in various parts of the British Isles.

Yachting.

Affiliated Member Clubs of the Royal Yachting Association:

Locality	*Club*
Ferry Beach, Barrow-in-Furness.	Barrow S.C.
Roa Island.	Roa Island B.C.
Coniston.	Coniston S.C.
Knott End.	Lancashire Schools Sailing & Canoeing Association.
Morecambe.	Morecambe & Heysham Y.C.
Morecambe Bay.	Morecambe Bay Sailing Assn.
River Lune and Glasson Basin.	Glasson S.C.
Skippool Creek, nr Fleetwood.	Blackpool and Fleetwood Y.C.

Dalton-in-Furness.

A Pace Egging Play is performed on Easter Saturday and Easter Monday; The play tours surrounding villages and is followed by the Ulverston Morris Dance. On Easter Saturday the play is performed in villages in Lakeland, while the Monday tour is confined to the Furness district. The route changes each year, though it is always performed in Dalton.

Good Friday.

Opening day for the hill climbers' and ramblers' year.

Lancaster.

Pace egging is held at Easter at the Easter Field, also known as the Giant Axe.

Ulverston.

The hound trailing season begins at Ulverston on Easter Monday. Hound trails are held two or three times a week from Easter to early November in the Furness district, Carnforth and the Lake District. Annual meets are usually held in connection with agricultural shows, and details of the weekly meets are announced in the local press. The hounds are slipped on the outskirts of a town or village, and race across moors and fells following a trail of aniseed which has previously been dragged over the course in an old sock.

Whittington, near Kirkby Lonsdale.

The Vale of Lune Harriers Hunt point to point. This is held on Easter Sunday at Low Hall Farm, Whittington; refreshments are available.

MAY

Cartmel.

Cartmel Races are held on Whit Saturday and Whit Monday; this is a steeplechase meeting in Cartmel Park. A hound trail takes place during the evening of Whit Saturday and all day Whit Monday.

Morecambe.

Although the Oceanarium and Aquarium at Marineland, More-cambe, is open throughout the year, from mid-May to October performing dolphins present several shows each day. Marineland exhibits include alligators, seals, penguins and tropical fish. Admission prices are 20p for adults and 10p for children (free if under five years).

During Morecambe Carnival Week, which coincides with the Spring Bank Holiday, various events of interest take place including a children's pet show and pony gymkhana. On the final Saturday a grand parade is held, the route being approximately 2¼ miles long. Morris dancers, entertaining troupes and carnival jazz bands from all parts of the north of England take part in the parade, and on reaching the carnival field compete for medals and cash prizes. On the field is a small fairground, special events including Cumberland style wrestling are held and refreshments are available.

Ulverston.

A Whitsuntide Hiring Fair is held in Ulverston for three days in Whit week at "The Gill" near the town centre. Although now taking the form of a pleasure fair, Mop Fairs or Hiring Fairs were once common throughout the country for the hiring of farm hands and servants.

JUNE

Lancaster.

Boundary Ridings are held in Lancaster every seven years. The last was in June, 1970, when Lancastrians, many mounted, set out to ride the old marks and bounds. The leader, wearing a leather apron, rings a bell as each point is reached. This man is called The Bellman, Lancaster being one of the few towns in Britain still retaining a Bellman. The mayor and town clerk accompany the ride, declaring the boundaries as they are reached.

JULY

Barrow-in-Furness.

The North Lonsdale Agricultural Show is held at Roosecote, Barrow-in-Furness, this one day show including many interesting local events.

Fleetwood to Morecambe Swim.

Organised by the Morecambe Cross Bay Swimming Association.

Grange-over-Sands.

The two-day Lakeland Rose Show takes place in Grange at the beginning of July. This is the largest rose show in the North-West and attracts exhibits from the leading rose growers of Great Britain. while there are also classes for sweet peas and flower arrangements. Admission prices are 30p for adults on the first day and 20p on the second day: there are reduced prices for children.

Lancaster.

The Admission of Freemen, a ceremony dating back over the centuries, occurs in July. Anyone resident in Lancaster for seven years and over 16 years of age can present himself at the Town Hall on a Saturday morning in mid-July to take the customary oath. For a fee of ten shillings, he promises to aid the Mayor and Corporation and keep the Queen's peace.

The Lancaster Regatta is held at Halton Waters, Lune Bank Gardens, Lancaster. There are two courses, the longer one from just below the M6 bridge and the shorter from approximately 200 yards beyond the aqueduct. The finish is towards the end of Lune Bank Gardens. The Regatta is organised by the City of Lancaster in conjunction with the John O' Gaunt Rowing Club and the Lancaster Royal Grammar School Boat Club. There are many races for both junior and senior competitors. Although this event has previously taken place in July, the possibility of holding the Regatta in May is under consideration.

Preston to Morecambe Carnival Run.

Veteran, vintage and post-vintage thoroughbred cars leave Preston during the morning, and after a fifty-mile run through the countryside arrive at Sandylands Promenade, Morecambe, at approximately mid-day. The cars travel along the Marine Road and take a simple driving test at the finishing point. The judging of the Concours d'Elegance takes place prior to the grand parade during the afternoon. The run is usually held on the second Sunday in July.

AUGUST

Broughton-in-Furness.

On August 1st, Charter Day is celebrated in Broughton. There is a declaration by the Bailiff charging everyone to keep the peace, and then coins are thrown to the children. The ceremony dates back to 1593.

The Broughton-in-Furness Show is held on the last Saturday in August; Hound trailing also takes place during the afternoon.

Carnforth.

The one-day Burton and Milnthorpe and Carnforth Agricultural Show takes place at Burton-in-Kendal, Carnforth.

Cartmel.

Cartmel Show is held on the first Wednesday in August; it features many Lakeland events including hound trailing. The summer Cartmel National Hunt Race Meeting is staged in Cartmel Park during the Summer Bank Holiday.

Grange-over-Sands.

The Grange and District Art Society's annual exhibition is to be seen in Grange during the first two weeks in August.

Kirkby Lonsdale.

Lunesdale Agricultural Society's one-day show is held at Underley Park.

Lancaster.

The Morecambe and Lancaster one-day agricultural show takes place at Cross Hill Park.

SEPTEMBER

Grange to Morecambe Cross Bay Swim.

The finals are held during the second week in September.

Hawkshead.

Hawkshead Agricultural Show is held on the first Tuesday in September; this is a one-day event which includes many local attractions.

Low Furness.

On the Sunday nearest St. Michael's Day, the Church of St. Michael and St. Mary at Urswick celebrates the annual rush bearing. Rushes are cut from the nearby tarn, and the children carry garlands and sheaves of the rushes called "bearings".

Lowick.

On the first Saturday in September a one-day agricultural show is held. This includes many local attractions, and hound trailing during the afternoon.

Opening of the season for Hunt Meets.

The North Lonsdale Foxhounds meet three times each week on Monday, Wednesday and Saturday. Those held in Lancashire include Lowick, Hawkshead, Coniston, Sawrey and Holker Hall. Meets begin at 9.30 a.m. up to November 21st, and 10 a.m. from then onwards. **The Vale of Lune Hunt** meets from September, usually twice a week on Wednesday and Saturday. Meets are at 11.30 a.m. and those held in Lancashire include Carnforth, Claughton, Bentham, Halton, Lowgill, Whittington, Arkholme and Wray. The kennels are at Hornby. **The Bleasdale Beagles,** the only pack in Lancashire, meet every Saturday from September to mid-March at Abbeystead, Trough of Bowland, Claughton-on-Brock, Chipping and other centres.

OCTOBER

Lancaster.

A season of international subscription concerts is held at Lancaster University from October to March. Details and tickets may be obtained from Messrs. Reddrop & Co. Ltd., 7 Frances Passage, Lancaster. The university also houses the Nuffield Theatre Group, run by the Nuffield Theatre Studio, and a number of plays are performed each year. Lancaster University is open to visitors, except for those parts where teaching is in progress or where students live.

The Eskdale and Ennerdale Foxhounds.

Meets are held from October to April, usually beginning at 9.30 a.m. Those in Lancashire include Broughton and the surrounding district.

NOVEMBER

Bolton-le-Sands.

During the winter months the Bolton-le-Sands group of the North Lancashire English Folk Dance and Song Society hold many social events including a barn dance.

Paythorne Bridge.

This bridge crosses the river Ribble in the Trough of Bowland. Crowds gather here on "Salmon Sunday," the Sunday nearest November 20th to watch for the arrival of the salmon.

Ulverston.

A Martinmas Hiring Fair is held on the same site as that in May. It lasts for three days and takes place in the week nearest to the 11th November.

MAPS:

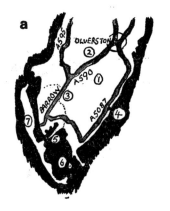

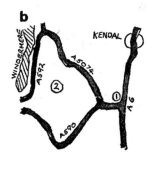

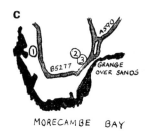

MORECAMBE BAY

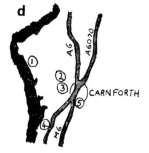

Maps *(continued)*

e

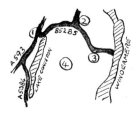

f

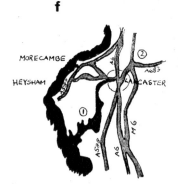

KEY TO MAPS:

A 1. Urswick
    2. Pennington
    3. Furness Abbey
    3. Aldingham
    5. Barrow Docks
    6. Piel Island
    7. Walney Island
B 1. Levens Hall
    2. Cartmel Fell Church
C 1. Holker Hall
    2. Cartmel Priory

    3. Cartmel Gatehouse
D 1. Silverdale, Trees
    2. Leighton Hall
    3. Warton Church
    4. Bolton-le-Sands Church
E 1. Coniston and Brantwood
    2. Hawkshead
    3. Sawrey
    4. Grizedale Forest
F 1. Overton Church
    2. Halton

Index:

Illustrations